D0370700

THE MODERN BACKPACKER'S HANDBOOK

THE
MODERN
BACKPACKER'S
HANDBOOK

Glenn Randall

LYONS & BURFORD, PUBLISHERS

Printed in the United States of America on 100% recycled paper of which 10% is derived from post-consumer waste.

Illustrations by Manuel F. Cheo

Design by Howard P. Johnson

10 9 8 7 6 5 4

Library of Congress Cataloging-in-Publication Data

Randall, Glenn, 1957–
    The modern backpacker's handbook / Glenn Randall.
        p. cm.
    Includes index.
    ISBN 1-55821-248-5
    1. Backpacking—Equipment and supplies.   I. Title.
GV199.62.R36   1993
796.5'1—dc20   ⸱ 93-37444
                                                         CIP

ACKNOWLEDGMENTS

First and foremost, I would like to thank my wife Cora for her companionship on the trail, her thoughtful comments on the manuscript and her patience with my initial resistance to many of her excellent suggestions. I would also like to thank my neighbors Gregg and Amy Thayer, wilderness guides and experienced parents of two lively daughters, for their comments on the chapter about hiking and backpacking with children.

CONTENTS

1 GEARING UP   13

2 OUTFITTING THE WELL-BURDENED CLOTHESHORSE   16

3 NO MEAN FEAT: BUYING BOOTS THAT WORK   28

4 PICKING A PACK THAT WORKS   39

5 THE TENTS DECISION: CHOOSING A WILDERNESS SHELTER   52

6 SLEEPING BAGS   63

7 BACKCOUNTRY STOVES   74

**8   MISCELLANEOUS
      ESSENTIALS**   81

**9   A PROVISIONAL GUIDE
      TO BACKCOUNTRY
      FOOD**   88

10   HITTING THE TRAIL   96

11   CLEAN CAMPING 101   121

**12   WILDERNESS
      KITCHENCRAFT**   140

**13   TAKING CARE OF
      SOME BODY—YOURS**   148

**14   WINTER: THE COOL
      ADVENTURE**   162

**15   BACKPACKING WITH
      CHILDREN**   173

**16   INVESTING YOURSELF
      IN WILDERNESS
      FUTURES**   180

APPENDIX   183

INDEX   186

INTRODUCTION

"I went to the woods because I wished to live deliberately, to front only the essential facts of life, and see if I could not learn what it had to teach, and not, when I came to die, discover that I had not lived."

—Henry David Thoreau, *Walden*, 1854.

Why go backpacking? Thoreau suggested one enduring answer. Backpacking is an antidote to industrialized society, where the pace of change accelerates constantly and buzzing swarms of tasks multiply exponentially, yet must be fitted into days that never grow longer. Every day, newspapers recite an endless dirge of war, poverty, oppression, and environmental disaster. Backpacking provides a temporary escape from life's complex and seemingly insoluble problems. In their stead, backpackers need only deal with a far more manageable set of concerns, each elemental in its simplicity: finding the easiest route, summoning the energy to walk that last mile, selecting a good campsite. Backpacking offers an abundance of life's most repeatable pleasures, the ones that never grow stale: resting when you're tired, eating when you're hungry, drinking when you're thirsty, and smashing a mosquito just before it bites.

To those basic pleasures, I would add two more, less connected with survival of the body than with survival of the spirit. The first is the quest for adventure. From one perspective, struggling mightily to reach a pass or the summit of a lofty mountain is absurd, possibly even mildly deranged; and yet, as the bumper sticker says, "If I wasn't nuts, I'd go insane." Sol Roy Rosenthal, M.D., has spent many years studying what he calls the "risk-exercise response," a powerful feeling of euphoria that follows participation in an adventurous sport. Dr. Rosenthal is quick to point out that he's not talking about life-threatening endeavors, but rather sports like skiing that contain an element of challenge, that cause participants to push themselves in some way, that provide some sense of venturing into the unknown. According to Rosenthal, the risk-exercise response goes beyond simply feeling good. Risk takers talk of living up to their potential, of feeling fulfilled and yet expecting more from their lives. For me, many of the hours I have spent hiking, climbing, and skiing in the wilderness stand out like lighthouse beacons in the night as I look back over the vast sea of undistinguished days that make up the bulk of my suburban life.

Finally, to the pleasures mentioned above, I would add the experience of profound beauty, an experience often intensified by strenuous effort. When I was thirteen, my father and I hiked up Strawberry Peak, one of the smaller peaks in the ring of mountains that almost encircles Los Angeles. As we were coming down, we crossed a creek. We knew that the trail led away from the creek for a spell, avoiding the deep canyon into which the creek disappeared, then crossed the creek again a mile or so farther down as the canyon walls diminished in height. To my boyish mind, the obvious proposition was irresistible: why not follow the creek through its dark and mysterious gorge? My father agreed, and we plunged in. All too soon, we discovered why the trail led around the canyon. The creek plunged over a 10-foot cliff, creating a lovely waterfall and a formidable obstacle to further progress. For a time we contemplated retracing our steps, but the day was old, and our legs had lost their spring. I spied a line of footholds and handholds tracing a possible route around the falls and began inching down, no doubt worrying my father tremendously. When I succeeded, he had to follow—which probably worried him even more. Overjoyed at our success, but wondering whether a larger, impassable waterfall lay just around the corner, we hurried around the next bend and discovered a marvelous limpid pool carved into the stone and filled to the brim by a bubbling cascade. I said to my father, "That's so perfect, it looks man-made."

He replied, in words that have stuck with me for more than twenty years, "That's the kind of perfection man strives to imitate."

Though two decades have elapsed since that simple hike, the

excitement of our little adventure and the small but stunning vision of beauty it offered are still the twin keys to my lifelong fascination with wilderness. There are no blank spots on the map anymore, no places marked "terra incognita," but there are still thousands of blank spots in my experience, thousands of peaks to climb and canyons to explore, thousands of wilderness vistas to feast upon with awestruck eyes. For me, no painting, sculpture, or photograph, no city, monument or building—nothing manmade—has ever compared to the beauty of nature at its grandest.

Backpackers don't set aside the twentieth century when they hoist their loads and head into the wilderness. Backpackers don't live off the land in any significant sense. If every backpacker cut his own bough bed, felled saplings to build a lean-to, and speared a porcupine for supper, the woods would become a wasteland in short order. In fact, far from spurning technology, backpackers frequently embrace it. The backpacking boom that began in the early 1970s was spurred on significantly by the application of sophisticated technology to the task of creating clothing, tents, stoves, and packs that could reasonably be carried on a bowed but unbroken human back. Necessarily, however, the use of technology is limited by backpacking's iron law: if you want it with you, you have to carry it. Some backpackers—perhaps all of them, at one time or another—become fascinated by the equipment game, minutely comparing the merits of one stove against another, one rain jacket against a second and third. Choosing gear that allows you to balance convenience, comfort, and utility with weight and bulk is an amusing sport, but one that ultimately misses the point. The heart and soul of backpacking can and should go much deeper than the love and mastery of gadgets.

The body of this book is filled with talk about gear and technique—practical information on how to be comfortable in the wilderness while leaving it untouched for the enjoyment of the next visitor. The soul of this book is the effort to instill a reverence for the wilderness that will allow low-impact hiking and camping practices to become second nature. Living simply in the woods is good practice for living in civilization. If we can learn to see the wilderness for what it is—a precious, fragile, irreplaceable treasure—then perhaps we can learn to see the whole world in the same light.

GEARING UP

"That man is richest whose pleasures are the cheapest."

—Henry Thoreau, *Journal*, 1856

I f you walk into a specialized outdoor shop and start pricing top-of-the-line gear as your first step toward going backpacking, you'll probably faint dead away and never set foot off pavement. Fortunately, there's no need to exhaust your bank account before you can start to enjoy the wilderness. For short day-trips in the summer, you probably have almost all the gear you need lying around the house. Sneakers are fine for your first outing, and for many more besides. Throw a wool sweater, a rain jacket, a water bottle, and some snacks into any old kind of book pack or day pack, and head out.

As you extend your range, you'll probably want some other items. More supportive, protective, and waterproof footwear will probably be one of your first purchases, and perhaps a more commodious and comfortable pack. You'll surely want a map of the area and a compass, if only to orient the map so it's facing north and so directions on the map correspond to directions on the ground.

Once you really get rolling, you'll probably get the itch to start investing in some of that lightweight high-tech gear whose prices once made your head swim. As you'll soon discover, it costs about $100 a pound to lighten your pack. Don't jump in headfirst, however, and end up buying gear that either doesn't work well or isn't exactly what you need. That's doubly expensive, because you'll probably keep hankering for the right gear until you finally cave in and buy it. Learn your way around before investing lots of money by talking to more experienced people, finding out what they like and don't like, then comparing their needs with yours.

Once you've put some trail miles behind you, it's time to start thinking about your first overnight trip. Many quality outdoor shops have rental programs that offer full-size packs, tents, sleeping bags and stoves. More experienced friends may be willing to lend you some gear for your first outing or two. You shouldn't have to make a big investment to try the sport for the first time.

GOING LIGHT

The quickest way to ruin your first trip is to overload your pack with too much stuff, then pick some ambitious itinerary requiring you to hike 30 miles and gain 5,000 feet of elevation every day. Packs invariably grow heavier as the day progresses. The key to enjoying backpacking is to pare the load as much as possible. Aim for no more than 40 percent of your body weight; less is always better. Get in the habit of weighing gear on a postage or bathroom scale and knowing approximately how much all of your gadgets and gizmos weigh. Learn what different pack weights feel like, and what you can reasonably carry in different types of terrain. A weight that can be carried easily on well-groomed trails can be as cantankerous as a cross-eyed mule if you're climbing, scrambling, bushwhacking, or on skis. "Take half of it and go for it" is the half-joking philosophy of mountaineering that is equally applicable to backpacking. With experience, you'll quickly find that you can do without many of the items you considered essential at first. Learn to leave behind all unnecessary gizmos.

Eventually, if backpacking really grabs you, you'll want to invest in your own gear instead of renting and borrowing. My philosophy on buying equipment was defined as a boy, when my dad told me to always buy good tools. "If you buy a lousy one," he said, "you'll curse it forever, but you'll never want to spend the money to buy a good one because you'll already have one that's marginally adequate." I try to define my needs carefully, buy the best I can afford, then take care of it meticulously and make it last. The cost of good gear, per year of use, is probably no higher than the cost of buying cheap gear and throwing it away when it breaks or falls apart after a year or two of service. When you factor in the satisfaction of using top-quality equipment, the investment begins to seem like a bargain.

The best place to find high-quality backpacking gear is undoubtedly at a specialty shop. Not only will the shop carry a good selection of the best gear, but the salespeople are likely to be knowledgeable about its strengths and weaknesses. Most specialty shops hire people who participate actively in a wide range of outdoor sports. They can often provide valuable suggestions on what will work best for your intended purpose. If there is no specialty shop in your area, consider buying from one of the big mail-order outfits like R.E.I., E.M.S. and L.L. Bean. Avoid the camping-supply sections of discount chains. The gear there may be cheap, but it will also be heavy, bulky and probably ineffective.

"Good gear," meaning lightweight, durable, effective gear, is undeniably expensive. But console yourself with the thought that once you have made the purchase, you can vacation at will while hardly spending more than you would if you were home and commuted to work every day.

OUTFITTING THE WELL-BURDENED CLOTHESHORSE

"Beware of all enterprises that require new clothes."

—Henry Thoreau, *Walden*

In July, not long ago, Cora and I were hiking in the popular Indian Peaks Wilderness near Denver when a powerful thunderstorm rolled in over Arapaho Pass. A hard rain began, which congealed quickly into stinging hail. Cora and I dove into our packs and pulled on the full rain suits—pants and jacket—that we carry on all but the shortest hikes, even at the height of summer. Shielded comfortably from the storm's depredations, we continued our hike, enjoying the wild peals of thunder and the staccato lightning bolts glimpsed through the trees.

Suddenly a couple in their early thirties appeared around a bend, heading for the parking lot a mile away as fast as they could run in their $2.97 flip-flops. Their shorts and T-shirts were already soaked through by the 35-degree rain and melting hail. The man carried a baby in a backpack, shielding it as best he could with the only piece of protective clothing they'd brought; a nylon windbreaker that was certainly not waterproof. We knew they would probably come out all right so long as neither of them seriously sprained an ankle on the slippery, muddy trail, but we both shook our heads at the unnecessary misery as we stood aside to let them pass.

While that incident was an extreme case, it was by no means the first time I'd seen poorly prepared summer hikers blown like chaff before the wrath of a Rocky Mountain thunderstorm. It's easy to forget, when you leave the plains on a blue-sky morning with a forecasted high of 85 degrees, that conditions in the mountains may be far different by 3:00.

SUMMER CLOTHING

Here's a quick list of the clothing Cora and I normally carry for summer backpacking in the Rockies: T-shirt, shorts and sun hat; a synthetic long-sleeve turtleneck; a hooded synthetic (not cotton) sweatshirt; synthetic long-john bottoms; a thick synthetic sweater; a warm hat (synthetic ski hat or pile-lined cap); light gloves; rain jacket; and rain pants. If we expect the mosquitoes to be out in force (and they usually are in most mountain regions in the summer), we'll throw in a lightweight, loose-fitting shirt and pair of pants. The sun hat I like is a baseball cap with a skirt that hangs down to my collar. The skirt keeps both sun and mosquitoes off my neck. A couple of companies currently make such "safari caps." If you don't want to buy one, you can fashion one yourself with a baseball cap, an old handkerchief or bandanna, and some safety pins. Cora adds a down jacket to this list to keep her warm during sunrise photo shoots. In the warm, humid climate of the central and southern Appalachians in summer, you certainly won't need this much clothing. In the northern Appalachians, the Rockies, the Pacific Northwest, and the Sierras, however, the amount we carry is probably about right for most people.

That clothing list leads immediately to another of Murphy's laws of backpacking: in good weather, the packs carried by well-prepared hikers will always seem inordinately large and heavy because they will be crammed with all the foul-weather gear that may be needed in a few short hours.

SUMMER CLOTHES

Let's take that list item by item and fill in a few details.

Despite all my warnings about being prepared for the worst, shorts certainly have their place in the mountains. I'm sure I've worn shorts for at least 75 percent of the summer miles I've ever hiked. I prefer tough, quick-drying nylon shorts rather than dressier cotton shorts that abrade quickly and soak up water like a camel. Shorts with pockets let you keep your lip balm and pocket knife handy; running shorts without pockets are less bulky and more comfortable if you wear them as underwear and keep them on when you slip on your long johns. Be careful if you wear shorts with an elastic waistband while carrying a heavy pack. The waistband's corrugated texture can chafe the small of your back, so I like to tuck my shirt inside my waistband to provide a little padding and protection against abrasion. A leather belt can be an even worse offender. Wear a soft nylon webbing belt, or choose shorts that don't need a belt to prevent them from becoming ankle hobbles.

Like shorts, a cotton T-shirt is mandatory for wearing on warm days, when cotton's absorbency is actually an advantage. First, cotton provides cool comfort if you're sweating while working hard. Second, cotton soaks up sweat so that when the weather does turn chilly, you can peel off your T-shirt, taking the sweat with it, and don a dry long-sleeve synthetic turtleneck over relatively dry skin. Hang the T-shirt on the outside of your pack and it will dry slowly, so long as it doesn't actually rain. With a little luck with the sunshine, it will dry enough that it won't feel like an ice cube the next time you put it on.

In many areas of the country, the next two items of clothing you'll want are loose-fitting long pants and a long-sleeve shirt to keep the bugs at bay. I say loose-fitting because mosquitoes bite readily through tight-fitting knitted long underwear. The ideal material for your bug pants is probably quick-drying polyester or nylon. Unfortunately, such pants can be hard to find and rather expensive. A cheap alternative is a pair of lightweight cotton or cotton/polyester pants that you can pick up at a discount department store. Just don't count on cotton pants to keep you warm if it rains. For that, you'll need a pair of synthetic long johns.

When the weather turns chilly, get out of your bug gear and start donning insulating garments. Insulation in clothing is actually provided mostly by the air trapped in between the fibers of the garment, not by the fibers themselves. Air conducts heat far more slowly than clothing fibers, which differ little among themselves in terms of their heat conductivity. Air's low heat conductivity makes the preservation of tiny air pockets critically important in an insulating garment.

No matter how well your garment traps air, its ability to insulate will still deteriorate if it gets wet, whether from rain or from perspiration. To quote equipment innovator and in-the-buff nature enthusiast Jack Stephenson, "Nothing is warm when wet but a hot tub." Evaporation of water from your skin extracts an enormous amount of heat. In addition, wet skin is just plain uncomfortable. Manufacturers of insulating garments have responded to this problem by devoting a great deal of energy to creating (and hyping) fabrics that are supposed to wick moisture away from your skin, leaving your skin drier and more comfortable. At least in theory, wicking should also reduce the rate at which you become chilled from evaporative cooling because the water will evaporate from the surface of the garment, well away from your skin, instead of directly from your skin itself.

FABRICS FOR BACKPACKING CLOTHING

Cotton is the worst wet-weather material. By its nature, cotton is a highly absorbent fiber that loses all its resiliency and springiness when it gets wet. This lack of wet-weather backbone causes all of the tiny air pockets that really provide your insulation to collapse and disappear. To make matters worse, water conducts heat about twenty times faster than dry air, ten times faster than dry cotton. If your cotton T-shirt or sweatshirt gets wet, you've got the worst of both worlds: no air pockets to provide insulation, and a dense mat of saturated, highly conductive fibers clinging to your skin and conducting heat like crazy. Water evaporates directly off your skin, increasing your frigid misery. To add a final insult, cotton clings tenaciously to the water it absorbs, so it dries very slowly.

Wool shares cotton's bad habit of sucking up water like a sponge, but it has one redeeming feature that made it the fiber of choice before synthetics: it retains its resiliency when wet. That means it traps tiny air pockets and won't collapse against your skin like cotton. But the problem with wool is that it dries just as slowly as cotton. If the sheep from which it came happened to have a particularly dyspeptic disposition, it also makes my skin itch and even break out in a rash. But if economy is your main criterion, you can probably pick up military-surplus woollies for a song. Just be aware that you may be singing the blues if they get wet the first day, because they'll probably stay wet for the rest of the trip.

Synthetics offer three significant advantages compared to cotton: they retain their resiliency and insulating capacity when wet; they absorb very little water; and they dry fast. In addition, synthetics are generally more abrasion-resistant than natural fibers, so they last longer. Polypropylene was the first synthetic to be widely used in outdoor clothing, but it has come under fire recently for its rather harsh, plastic feel, its penchant for shrinking into doll clothes if thrown into the clothes dryer, and its tendency to embrace body odors and refuse to let them go, even under threat of repeated washing in paint thinner. Polyester seems to be the material of choice now for long underwear and for the large and varied assortment of thick, heavily napped fabrics loosely called pile or fleece. Polyester can be knitted into lightweight, wonderfully soft and comfortable styles for long underwear and bulkier forms for sweaters and jackets. It doesn't cling to odors as much as polypropylene and bears up well under normal washing and drying. Nylon, while ubiquitous as the shell fabric in rain gear and insulated parkas because of its great strength and abrasion resistance, is rarely used in insulating clothes, with one exception. Several manufacturers are using bicomponent fabrics which have a rapid-wicking, nonabsorbent polyester inner layer and an absorbent nylon outer layer. The intent is to create a "push-pull" effect that draws moisture off your skin through the wicking action of the polyester, then pulls it into the nylon, which is specially treated to be highly absorbent. In my experience, these hydrophobic/hydrophilic fabrics certainly make my skin feel drier than the other polyester underwear fabrics I've used.

LAYERING

As you begin building your collection of insulating clothing, think in terms of layers, a concept for which we are indebted to the late Benjamin Thompson, a.k.a. Count Rumford. Rumford, to quote one biographer, was an "unprincipled opportunist, a ruthless self-promoter and overbearingly arrogant." He was also, history tells us, the discoverer in the 1780s that the insulating property of clothing comes primarily from trapped air. From this he concluded that several thin layers of clothing were warmer than one thick one because they trapped air in between the layers as well as within the layers themselves. Carrying several thin layers, rather than one thick layer, has an additional advantage: it gives you the flexibility to fine-tune the amount of clothing you're wearing to match your heat output and the current temperature exactly. If you bring just a heavy parka and a T-shirt, you might have the same total amount of insulation available to you as if you brought two thin shirts and a sweater, but in a very inconvenient form. With no ability to have just a medium amount of insulation, you'll probably be too hot wearing the parka or too cold wearing just the T-shirt.

For summer use in the mountains of the Lower 48, one layer of synthetic underwear for your legs is usually plenty while hiking. For lounging around camp, a second layer of synthetic underwear can be nice, or you can layer your mosquito pants or rain pants (or both) over your long johns for a surprising amount of additional warmth. For my torso, I like to bring a synthetic turtleneck with a neck zipper for ventilation, a fleece sweatshirt, and a fleece sweater to provide some versatility in layering. If you can't find a synthetic sweatshirt, I suggest bringing a second turtleneck shirt plus a neck gaiter—a knitted or pile fabric tube that you pull over your head and wear around your neck. The hood on my sweatshirt and the neck gaiter serve the same purpose: insulating your neck, which is well supplied with blood vessels that run near the surface. These vessels, with their cargo of warm blood, provide a large escape hatch for heat. In cold weather, it pays to insulate them well. To insulate my head, I usually carry a pile ski hat as well. Lately I've also begun carrying a waterproof/breathable baseball cap with ear flaps to keep my hair dry in the rain.

Pile comes in many varieties today. Fortunately, the performance in terms of drying speed and resiliency when wet doesn't vary a whole lot. Warmth does vary with thickness. After deciding on what thickness you need, choose your pile jacket based on fit and overall attractiveness. Look for a full-length front zipper that lets you ventilate easily. Hand-warmer pockets are welcome on cool mornings, and a zippered pocket or two is handy for keeping small valuables accessible. If you're really cold-blooded, like Cora, you should consider adding pile pants to your summer layering system. Look for a pair that has full-length zippers along the outside of the pant legs. Better yet, look for a pair with side zippers that separate at the top next to the waistband, so in the wintertime you can put them on without taking off your skis or snowshoes.

RAIN GEAR

The outermost layer in your summer clothing arsenal should always be some solidly built rain gear. I am still dumbfounded at the number of times I've seen people with a cotton sweatshirt tied around their waist blithely heading upward above timberline as a vicious squall gathers strength and begins bearing down on its clueless victims.

The least expensive rain gear is a plastic poncho, a large square of vinyl with a hole in the middle capped with a hood. Unfortunately, ponchos are useful only in brief, gentle rains not accompanied by wind—a description that doesn't fit the typical high-mountain thunderstorm. In a real thunderstorm, a poncho's loose, floppy fabric is guaranteed to billow up around your face with the first gust, leaving you blinded and stumbling while the wind-driven horizontal rain soaks everything below your shoulders. Don't waste your money on a glorified tablecloth, no matter how cheap it seems; you'll want something better almost immediately.

The next step above a poncho is a rain jacket made of urethane-coated nylon. These garments are waterproof if their seams are sealed and the coating hasn't worn away under the abrasion of your pack straps, but they allow sweat to escape only at the cuffs, neck, and waist—not through the fabric itself. If you wear such nonbreathable rainwear while you're inactive (fishing, swearing at fishing, swearing off fishing forever, etc.), then it performs adequately. If you're active, however, it's difficult to prevent sweat from building up inside your rain gear and soaking your insulating layers. When hiking hard in nonbreathable rain gear, you face two ugly options: get soaked by sweat, or remove your rain gear and get soaked by rain.

This eternal dilemma has spurred the development of more than a dozen fabrics that claim to be both waterproof and breathable. The first was Gore-Tex. Since this is the first time this modern "miracle fabric" has surfaced in this book, it seems fitting to offer a brief explanation to those of you who haven't yet been exposed to W. L. Gore's advertising avalanche. In truth, Gore-Tex is pretty nifty stuff. By all reasonable standards, Gore-Tex is indeed impenetrable by liquid water; by most reasonable standards, in most situations, Gore-Tex does indeed breathe, allowing moisture in the form of water vapor to escape from your sweaty body. This miracle is achieved by the construction of a two-layer composite. One layer is made of expanded poly-tetrafluoroethylene, PTFE for short, better known as Teflon. This material is laced with 9 billion pores per square inch. These pores are larger than the water molecules found in water vapor, but bigger than a droplet of liquid water. The second layer, whose name is even more unpronounceable and therefore seldom mentioned in polite society, is a nonporous film of polyalkylene oxide polyurethane-urea that absorbs water molecules on the warm, humid side of the material, next to your body, and discharges those molecules on the drier, cooler side away from your body. The Gore-Tex membrane "breathes" when the temperature and humidity on the inside of the fabric next to your body is greater than the temperature and humidity on the outside of the fabric. In most situations where you want to be wearing rain gear or other Gore-Tex garments, such conditions prevail.

Waterproof/breathable fabrics go a long way toward soothing the hiker's problem, but don't expect miracles. All waterproof/breathable fabrics have limitations. Sweat can escape only in vapor form. If it's extremely cold and your sweat condenses into liquid droplets before it reaches the inside of your jacket, the moisture will remain trapped inside your clothing. Sweat can also escape only if the temperature and humidity inside your garment is higher than the temperature and humidity outside. If you're working hard during a steamy Georgia thunderstorm, your rain gear probably won't seem very breathable. For a time, manufacturers of waterproof/breathable fabrics seemed intent on waging an MVTR war, with legions of shock troops rolling out statistics on the Moisture Vapor Transport Rate of their fabrics. The MVTR is usually expressed in terms of the number of grams of moisture that can pass through a square meter of fabric in 24 hours under specified conditions of temperature and humidity. Things have gotten pretty quiet on that front lately, partly because every manufacturer had his own test, which made it impossible to compare results among different manufacturers, partly because it was pretty hard for consumers to relate the test results to the real world, and partly because Gore-Tex seemed to be winning the war and the other manufacturers decided to shut up and cut their losses. Suffice it to say, however, that even the most breathable fabrics can only pass a certain amount of moisture per hour. If I go running during a Colorado thunderstorm, I often find upon my return that the inside of my rain jacket is damp. The jacket feels as if it leaked; but when I test the fabric with a device that forces water against the fabric under pressure, I find that the material is still waterproof. It simply can't breathe fast enough to dispel the amount of moisture I produce during very vigorous exercise. You can enhance the breathability of your rainwear during rainstorms if you maintain the surface water repellency of the fabric. All rain gear comes with a water-repellent treatment applied to the outer surface of the fabric. This treatment is distinct from whatever method the manufacturer uses to make the fabric waterproof. The water-repellent treatment causes water to bead up on the jacket's surface. Once that treatment wears off, water tends to coat the jacket's surface in an even film. That coating of water chills the fabric by evaporation, which promotes condensation inside the jacket. The coating may also reduce breathability. The water repellency of your jacket can be renewed by applying various grocery-store products like Scotchgard. According to W. L. Gore, the best products are based on a fluoropolymer, not silicone. Read the instructions and list of ingredients on the can before buying.

Like breathability, waterproofness is a relative term. Here the statistics are usually given in terms of pounds per square inch (psi) of water pressure that the fabric will withstand. According to W.L. Gore & Associates, makers of Gore-Tex, a 165-pound man kneeling on wet ground is pushing water against the fabric of his rain pants with a force of about 16 pounds per square inch (psi). When he's sitting, he's exerting a pressure of about 3 psi. The military standard for waterproofness is 25 psi. Some manufacturers give the waterproofness of their fabric in terms of the height of a column of water that the fabric will withstand. ("Our fabric will withstand a column of water four meters high!") While these numbers may sound impressive, actually they're not. A water column 4 meters high, for example, exerts a pressure of less than 6 psi. That's adequate for a ski garment exposed only to falling snow, but pretty marginal as summer rain gear, particularly when you consider that waterproofness generally declines with repeated washings.

Despite all these caveats, waterproof-breathable rain gear is still a major improvement over nonbreathable gear. In my opinion, Gore-Tex is probably still the best waterproof-breathable. Its competitors are generally either less breathable, or less waterproof, or both. Gore-Tex is admittedly expensive (somebody's got to pay for all that advertising), but most hikers and backpackers seem to have decided that it's worth its cost.

Gore-Tex is used in clothing in several different constructions. In three-layer construction, the Gore-Tex membrane is glued to both an inner and outer fabric. In two-layer construction, the membrane is glued only to the outer fabric; the lining fabric, which is essential to protect the membrane, hangs free. Three-layer Gore-Tex jackets are more durable but stiffer than two-layer. The breathability of the two constructions is about the same. A Gore-Tex membrane can also be laminated to a layer of mesh fabric that hangs inside the outer shell of the garment. This is referred to as LTD construction, which stands for "laminated to the drop-liner." LTD construction is primarily used in apparel for highly aerobic sports like running because it's a bit more breathable than traditional two-layer and three-layer construction. It's rarely used in rain gear because the outer layer of fabric can soak through easily. In a fourth style, called Z-liner construction, the Gore-Tex membrane is laminated to a mesh fabric that hangs between the liner and the outermost shell fabric. Z-liner construction is primarily used in fashion pieces designed for the city. For the most part, I prefer three-layer construction for its durability.

I used to believe that only a rain jacket was really needed, and that rain pants were an unnecessary weight and expense. Then, like the people I now decry, I foolishly pushed for the summit of 14,255-foot Longs Peak one August day a number of years ago, disregarding the approaching thunderstorm. The wind-driven horizontal rain, hail and snow immediately saturated my long johns. The evaporative cooling from my legs was so strong that no amount of dry, rain-jacket protected insulation on my torso could keep me warm. A few years later, having inadequately learned my lesson, I asked Jeff Lowe, one of America's most experienced Himalayan mountaineers, whether he was going to bring rain pants when we tried a climb on Longs' formidable east face. I assumed that a tough guy like Jeff, intent on going fast and light, would eschew such frippery as rain pants. "I always bring them," he replied. I did so, too, and was glad—we were hammered by a severe thunderstorm only halfway up the peak and were forced to retreat. I've brought rain pants on mountain ventures ever since, whether I'm off to do a difficult climb or just take a stroll up to a beautiful lake.

You could do worse than to select your rain jacket on the basis of how well you like the hood design. In general, I prefer integral hoods that are sewn permanently to the jacket because they're easier to pull up over your head, particularly while wearing gloves in a high wind. The alternative is a detachable hood that usually stows in a pocket in the collar. Detachable hoods stay on your head in the wind only if you fasten two flaps across your chin with Velcro or snaps, a feat that can be awkward while wearing gloves. Stuffing the hood into the pocket on the collar usually turns the collar into a cervical brace—fine if you're planning on rolling your truck in a crash on the way to the trail head, not so great for comfortable hiking.

In most situations, you'll be wearing a pack over your rain jacket, so make sure that your pack's shoulder straps and waist belt don't cover up the pocket openings. Be sure, too, that the contents of the pockets can't drop down beneath the waist belt, where they can chafe and jab.

INSULATED PARKAS

Cora brings a down jacket on every mountain backpacking trip, even in August, and wears it regularly during early breakfasts and late dinners. In the summer, I find I stay warm enough without one if I put on my rain pants and jacket to block the wind and trap warm air. In the winter, I normally bring a down jacket. If you do decide you need an insulated parka, your first choice involves the type of fill. Since you'll face the same choice in an even more important context when you buy a sleeping bag, I'll hit the subject lightly here and go into more depth in Chapter 6.

For years, chemists have sought a synthetic equivalent to down, the innermost plumage of ducks and geese. So far, nothing they have produced an equal high-quality down on the basis of insulating capacity for a given weight. Good down is also more compressible than the best synthetics, which saves room in your pack. While down costs more than synthetics initially, it retains its loft longer, so the cost per year is usually less if you take good care of the shell fabric. On the negative side, down, like cotton, loses all its resiliency when it gets wet. A wet down jacket is as worthless as a pack of used bubble gum, and it's likely to remain worthless until you get a day of brilliant sunshine or drop a lot of quarters in the nearest Doozy Duds clothes dryer. Synthetic insulators retain their loft when wet and dry much faster.

Slowly, over the years, the synthetics have been catching up in the warmth-for-weight category. At present, Lite Loft, a blend of polyester and polyolefin fibers, seems to be the closest contender, even rivaling low-grade down in some tests. However, Lite Loft has not yet withstood the test of time, and some flaw may become apparent that limits its appeal. Polarguard, a continuous filament polyester fiber, and Quallofil, a loose bunch of short polyester fibers, are also found in insulated jackets.

My preference in parka insulation has been honed by my experiences in the wintertime Rockies and in the high, glaciated mountains of the Alaska Range. For those climates, which are very cold and relatively dry, I prefer down, particularly if protected by a Gore-Tex shell. In the wetter climate of the Northwest and Northeast, and in coastal Alaska and Canada, a synthetic-filled parka is probably a better bet.

USEFUL ACCESSORIES

A few clothing odds-and-ends can help make the trip more pleasant. To prevent gravel from falling in the top of your boots, you

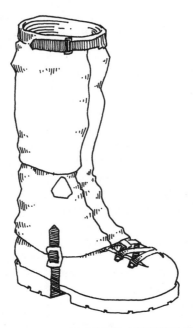

GAITERS KEEP SNOW, ROCKS, AND DIRT OUT
OF YOUR BOOTS.

can wear a pair of gaiters: fabric tubes that cover the upper portion of your boots and extend up your calves. A strap that goes under your instep prevents the gaiter from riding up. Most gaiters use Velcro or a zipper—sometimes combined with snaps—to make it easy to fasten the tube of fabric around your calf. Short gaiters reaching just above the anklebone are sufficient to keep gravel out of the tops of your shoes. Longer gaiters reaching to just below your knee are essential in deep snow to keep snow out of your boots and to keep your pant legs dry. A few people wear knee-high gaiters in desert areas to protect their calves from thorny plants.

In high mountain areas, light gloves are a must, even in summer. Early mornings, particularly, can be quite chilly on the fingers when handling stoves, pots and pans and camera gear. I like cross-country ski gloves with leather palms and fingers and a knitted fabric back. Knitted polypropylene or polyester gloves also work well, but they get wet faster and aren't as durable. Polypropylene gloves will melt if you use them to pick up hot pots.

Although it may horrify some city folks to think about it, back-packers rarely bring a fresh change of clothes for each day of the trip. Socks are one exception; a fresh pair of cotton or nylon briefs is another (although I usually wear my nylon shorts, which have a sewn-in brief, as underwear). Cora brings an extra synthetic long underwear top, both for the pleasure of wearing a fresh-smelling garment partway into the trip, and for the option it gives her to doff a sweat-soaked shirt and put on a dry one when the wind starts to blow.

Like street clothing, outdoor garb comes with care instructions printed on a tag that's sewn to the garment. Fortunately, caring for the latest generation of outdoor clothing is usually simple. Gore-Tex, for example, can be machine-washed in warm water and dried on warm in an ordinary home dryer. W. L. Gore recommends against dry cleaning, bleach, and fabric softeners. As strange as it may sound, you can renew some types of water-repellent treatments on shell gear by careful ironing. Check your jacket's garment tag or hangtag for specifics. Most of the popular polyester fleeces and long-underwear fabrics can also be machine-washed and dried gently. Down- and synthetic-filled parkas should be hand-washed or washed in a large-capacity *front-loading* washing machine. See Chapter 6 for more details.

After reading over 5,000 words on the subject of backpacking attire, you could certainly be forgiven for agreeing with Thoreau's admonition to "beware of all enterprises that require new clothes." But take heart: if you're like me, you'll soon find that the new clothes you buy for backpacking are so practical, durable, and comfortable that they quickly become the old clothes you wear all the time, whether or not you're in the wilderness.

NO MEAN FEAT:
BUYING BOOTS THAT WORK

"The Pobble who has no toes
Had once as many as we;
When they said, "Some day you may lose
  them all"—
He replied, "Fish fiddle de-dee!"

—Edward Lear, *The Pobble Who Has No Toes*, 1877

I t was time for my wife Cora to buy her first pair of cross-country ski boots. I well remembered my own first pair: cheap, low-cut and poorly insulated, which contributed to the frostnip I suffered on my little toes during one particularly stormy ski tour along the Continental Divide. The boots' injection-molded soles eventually broke in half in the middle of a 12-mile tour. I vowed Cora would not repeat that mistake. Instead, she would buy top-quality boots to start with, saving money in the long run because she wouldn't buy cheap boots that would only be discarded after a year.

So she bought a beautiful pair of heavy-duty black telemark boots, costing over $300: they kept her feet warm, supported her ankles perfectly—and gave her the worst case of blisters I'd ever seen. She had bought too much boot.

My first pair of hiking boots, purchased twenty years ago, performed the same atrocities on my heels. Constructed entirely of stout leather with massive, heavily lugged soles, those ancient millstones weighed as much as the modern plastic boots I've worn on the summit of 20,320-foot Mount McKinley when it was 20° below. An old army adage holds that a pound on your feet is equivalent to five pounds on your back in terms of the energy you must exert while walking. To add insult to injury and exhaustion, the boots were so stiff that they made me walk like a one-year-old with fused ankles. In reaction to those cement-block blister boxes, I then spent most of the next fifteen years scampering around the summertime mountains in various pairs of running shoes. True, they afforded little protection and got wet easily, but they were light, comfortable and never gave me blisters. If you aren't prone to spraining your ankles and you plan to hike on dry summertime trails with a light load, there's not much wrong with running shoes. Just make sure they have enough tread left to prevent you from slipping on gravel.

LIGHTWEIGHT BOOTS

Once you start carrying significant weight, however, you'll need footwear that provides more support. Fortunately, running-shoe technology has taken over the lightweight-boot market. Today, store shelves groan beneath boots whose uppers are constructed of panels of Cordura nylon and thin, lightweight pieces of leather. The upper is glued to the midsole and outsole using the same techniques that are used in running-shoe construction. The result is an inexpensive, reasonably durable boot that offers some degree of ankle protection and support. Best of all, fabric/leather hiking boots require almost no break-in time. Low-cut models whose uppers end below the ankle-bone weigh less and give you greater ankle flexibility than higher-cut models, but don't provide enough protection and support for back-packing with heavy loads.

A TYPICAL LIGHTWEIGHT, LEATHER HIKING
BOOT.

Lightweight boots have another advantage: they help reduce trail erosion. The heavily lugged soles that were always a part of the massive waffle-stompers of the 1970s did an effective job of chewing up soft trail surfaces, particularly trails crossing loamy soils back East. When the next rainstorm arrived, the trails were primed to erode. Most of the new generation of lightweight boots have smaller lugs which make shallower imprints in the trail. That means less dirt that's primed to head downhill with the first rain drops. It also means that trailside vegetation gets a break. On many trails, it's hard to argue that a hefty boot is really necessary. Legendary Grandma Gatewood hiked the Appalachian Trail three times, starting at age sixty-seven, wearing Keds sneakers. For the sake of your leg muscles and the sake of the trail, buy the lightest boot you feel you can get away with. Or, if you feel you must have a heavy boot for carrying a heavy load or to protect weak ankles, consider bringing a pair of running shoes or sandals to wear around camp, where the impact of hikers on vegetation is often highest.

The failure points of fabric/leather hiking boots are the seams and the lining fabric. As veteran boot repairman Steve Komito puts it, "Every place where you've got a seam, you've got a place where the boot can come apart." Fabric/leather hiking boots have a lot of seams. To ameliorate this problem you can apply some kind of liquid sealant or boot-patching compound to the seams to make them more abrasion resistant. No brand I've tried seems to resist peeling for more than a month or two, however, so I'll leave you on your own to explore the boot shop's shelves for the latest and greatest. A boot repairman may be able to restitch a boot that's returning to its component pieces.

There's not much you can do to prevent the lining fabric from wearing out, and nothing a boot repairman can do to fix the problem, either. If the lining fabric is worn to the point where it's giving you blisters, it's time for new boots. Most boots can be resoled, but the uppers are usually in such bad shape by the time the soles are worn out that it's rarely worth the trouble.

KEEPING YOUR FEET DRY

Fabric/leather hiking boots are ubiquitous on dry summer trails, but that doesn't mean they're perfect. Their central weakness is that they're scarcely more waterproof than a pair of running shoes, and there's no practical way to waterproof them for very long. You can apply various wax-based waterproofing compounds to the leather, which will enhance their waterproofness for a time, but there's nothing that's comparably effective that you can do to the nylon. Silicone sprays, which some manufacturers recommend, last for about a day or less.

The easiest, cheapest solution is an end run. Give up on trying to keep your *boots* dry; instead, keep your *socks* and *feet* dry by wearing plastic bags over your socks. True, the bags only last a day and then become worthless. A higher-tech solution is to buy vapor-barrier socks made of waterproof coated nylon or, even fancier, the waterproof/breathable Gore-Tex socks currently offered by at least one supplier.

When I obtained my first pair of Gore-Tex socks, I tested them by going running on some very wet, snowy, and muddy trails. I put a polypropylene liner sock on both feet, then donned a waterproof but nonbreathable vapor-barrier sock on one foot, a Gore-Tex sock on the other. During the run, I didn't notice any difference in the temperature of my feet. The Gore-Tex didn't breathe enough to provide noticeable evaporative cooling. When I finished my run, however, I noticed that the Gore-Tex-clad foot was considerably drier than the foot encased in the nonbreathable waterproof sock. I found the same pattern when I compared nonbreathable waterproof gaiters to Gore-Tex gaiters while snowshoeing. One caution: The Gore-Tex socks I wore add significant bulk, making my boots feel somewhat tighter. You may need to wear a thinner sock combination to allow room for the Gore-Tex socks.

Gore-Tex is also incorporated permanently into the linings of many fabric/leather hiking boots in the form of a seam-sealed Gore-Tex bootie. In my experience, Gore-Tex is a highly valuable addition to a fabric/leather boot. In one test I conducted, I immersed several pairs of Gore-Tex boots in three inches of water for four hours. None of them admitted a drop. Then I tested a nearly-new all-leather hiking boot without a Gore-Tex liner. At the end of four hours, I poured half a cup of water out of the boot.

Despite that discouraging result, all-leather hiking boots that rely strictly on the waterproofness of their leather to keep your feet dry are making a comeback. If given regular applications of a waterproofing compound, well-made models that use good leather are certainly far more water-resistant than any non-Gore-Tex fabric/leather boot. All-leather boots also last much longer than fabric/leather boots because good leather is more abrasion-resistant than fabric. Every thread in a woven fabric comes to the surface. Break one thread, and you've got a hole. Leather's densely matted fibers tolerate much more abuse. In addition, bootmakers using leather can cut the upper from a single seamless piece. A boot with a one-piece upper will outlast any boot that's pieced together, whether the pieces are leather or fabric. All-leather boots usually provide much better support when you're hiking with a heavy load and have a certain time-honored aesthetic appeal. Application of the same running-shoe technology that allowed the creation of lightweight fabric/leather boots has also stripped pounds off the weight of the new all-leather boots. A few all-leather models back up their leather with a Gore-Tex liner, providing two barriers against the wet world outside. However, all-leather boots cost considerably more than fabric/leather boots.

As you extend your mountain hiking season into spring and fall, you'll find that waterproof boots become more and more important. In the spring, in any mountain range that gets significant winter snowfall, the trails become mud-banked rivers filled with icy snowmelt. In the fall, early storms often dump just a few inches of snow that makes the footing cold and soggy. Waterproof footwear not only keeps your feet dry, it allows you to stay on the trail rather than walking around the wet spots, which widens the trail and promotes erosion. I'll have more to say on this in Chapter 10.

WINTER BOOTS

If your hiking takes you out when the temperatures are much below freezing, you'll want to consider two other categories of footwear: pac boots and what I'll call winter hiking boots.

Boot guru Steve Komito's shop once displayed a sign that read; "Double boots are cheap—only $20 per toe." The sign, which was promoting ultrawarm boots consisting of an outer shell and a heavily insulated inner boot, was aimed at winter mountaineers and Himalayan aspirants. Its message, however, is equally applicable to anyone who goes out in frigid weather: insulated, waterproof footwear is worth the price—especially considering that the price of inadequate winter footgear may be frostbite. After all, he who dies with the most toes wins.

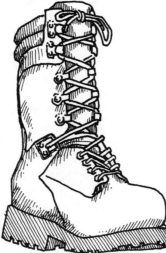

HIGH-TOPPED WINTER HIKING BOOTS
USUALLY HAVE FOAM INSULATION OR
THINSULATE.

A TYPICAL PAC BOOT HAS A MOLDED
RUBBER BOTTOM STITCHED TO A LEATHER
OR CORDURA TOP.

Pac boots have an all-leather or leather-and-fabric upper stitched to a molded rubber bottom. A removable liner, usually made of wool or polypropylene felt, provides insulation. Wool liners cost less; polypro liners dry faster. For equivalent thickness, the warmth is about the same. Pac boots are warmer than winter hiking boots—sometimes too warm—and totally waterproof up to the top of the molded rubber. They're water-resistant above that. Pac boots are instantly comfortable, requiring no break-in time, but the fit is usually rather sloppy because the insulation compresses under your foot and the boots are normally available only in full sizes. When fitting a pair, make sure that the top edge of the molded rubber doesn't jab you under the ankle bone while traversing a slope.

Pac boots are perfect for aurora watching and other inactive pursuits. For strenuous hiking or snowshoeing in rough terrain, where you want a snugger fit and better ankle support, look for a pair of insulated, waterproof winter hiking boots. They'll lighten your wallet more than pac boots, but also lighten the load on your feet.

Many of these boots are marketed as hunting boots because they're targeted to the hook-and-bullet crowd, but don't let the name put you off. Hunters spend a lot of time walking off-trail in cold, snowy, or marshy terrain, and they need warm, waterproof footwear more than most backpackers. Cold-weather hiking boots have all-leather or fabric and leather uppers that are stitched, cemented, or attached via injection molding to a stout lugged sole. All three construction techniques, including injection molding, which has been much improved in recent years, produce a durable boot. All-leather uppers typically cost more, weigh more, and last longer. The insulation, which is stitched permanently into the boot lining, is usually Thinsulate, a microfiber batting that resists compression and provides a lot of warmth with minimum thickness. Some manufacturers use various closed-cell foams as insulation, which don't provide quite as much warmth as Thinsulate for equivalent thickness. By general consensus among manufacturers, silicone-tanned or silicone-impregnated leathers are the most waterproof. Keeping leather waterproof is tough, however, and all boots need regular applications of boot waterproofing to retain their water repellency. As with summer hiking boots, the best insulated winter hiking boots back up their leather with a sewn-in Gore-Tex bootie.

BOOTS FOR WET SUMMER HIKING

There's one other category of footwear to consider: boots for warm, wet conditions, such as you find while hiking in the summer in those rare canyons in the Southwest that have permanently flowing streams. In many places, these streams *are* the trails; the banks are so choked with brush (and sometimes poison ivy) or hemmed in so tightly by cliffs that the only way to make progress is to walk right in the streambed. As a general rule, I dislike letting my feet remain wet for long periods. Waterlogged skin softens and blisters easily and is susceptible to fungal infections. On the other hand, the thought of wearing knee-high rubber boots on a 100° July day in southern Utah is equally repugnant. River-runners usually wear some kind of heavy-duty sandals that strap on securely so they won't wash away in rapids. Some models even have soles made of the same sticky, high-friction rubber used on rock-climbing boots. Sandals offer the advantage that they let your feet dry out quickly once you do get back onshore, but they provide no ankle support and no protection against bruising by hidden underwater rocks and branches. Other people like the low-cut rubber booties currently made by Nike for water sports, but I can't imagine myself hauling around a substantial pack in footwear with all the support of ballroom slippers. The best solution, I think, is to wear lightweight fabric/leather hiking boots with thin, nonabsorbent socks made of polypropylene, nylon or polyester. Once you're done with streamwalking for the day, change into dry socks and sandals or a lightweight pair of camp shoes.

FITTING BOOTS

The advent of supple, easily broken-in fabric/leather boots and lightweight all-leather boots has alleviated much of the anxiety that used to accompany boot shopping. In the past, the prospective victim trembled and asked himself: Will I ever be able to break these monsters in? Will I curse myself for years for purchasing an exorbitantly expensive pair of blister machines? Fortunately for backpackers, those days of fear and loathing are mostly gone. Still, a few words on fitting boots may be in order.

For starters, buy the socks you intend to wear before selecting your boots. The particular sock combination you choose affects the fit of your boots a great deal. As a general rule, I recommend wearing one pair of thin synthetic liner socks with a thicker pair of wool or wool-blend socks on top. The slick synthetic fibers of the liner sock tend to reduce friction and hold blisters at bay; the thick wool sock provides insulation and cushioning and absorbs moisture. Cotton socks are very comfortable if your feet will stay dry. If they get wet, however, cotton socks will lose their resiliency, collapse against your skin, and cling there, making your feet cold and clammy. Cotton is highly absorbent, which means it takes forever to dry. Some people recommend wearing silk liner socks because they believe that silk socks reduce blisters. Although they don't seem to help Cora, they might help you. I rarely have problems with blisters, so I can't speak to that claim from personal experience.

Once you've purchased the socks you'll be wearing, start trying on boots. In the past, when the lightweight boot revolution first hit, the hiker's decision was simple: which boot is lightest? Now that revolution has reached a plateau, and the hiker faces a different decision: what balance of weight versus support do I want? The ultralight boot that feels as comfortable as a running shoe in the store (because that's basically what it is) may leave your feet bruised and battered after 10 heavily laden miles.

Boots are made on a last, a metal form that defines the shape of the boot. Different manufacturers use different lasts; some narrow, some wide, depending on what they think will fit the greatest number of feet. A few manufacturers offer different widths in the same size and model of boot. Don't accept the first pair that feels vaguely right. Try different models and different manufacturers, and even different stores, which may carry styles the first did not. Unlace the boot completely and shove your foot as far forward as possible, until your toes touch the front of the boot. If you can fit one finger in between your heel and the back of the boot, the length is about right. Lace up the boot and walk. Does your heel shift up and down inside the boot? A small amount of movement may be acceptable, particularly in a stiff new boot. If the movement is excessive, however, it will cause blisters. Look for enough room at the front of the boot to "play piano with your toes," especially if you're buying a cold-weather boot. Snug boots restrict

MOUNTAINEERING BOOTS

Backpackers who leave the valley-bottom trails in pursuit of high summits will sooner or later find themselves confronting a steep, hard-packed snowfield. Dealing with such terrain isn't hiking anymore: it's mountaineering, with all of the dangers that that implies. Gravity works with surprising speed, and a slip not checked immediately on a 45° snowfield quickly becomes as unstoppable as a free-fall off a vertical cliff. Mountaineering places a whole new set of demands on judgment, skill, experience, and equipment. If you're interested in learning about mountaineering, seek expert instruction first, then begin upgrading your gear.

Among the new items you'll need are a pair of mountaineering boots that can be fitted with crampons, the spiked steel frames that climbers attach to their boots to gain traction on snow and ice. Some old-fashioned crampons lash on with neoprene straps. Modern crampons clamp on with a mechanism that's reminiscent of a much-simplified alpine ski binding. To accommodate the pressures generated by attaching crampons, mountaineering boots must have rigid soles and stout uppers. That makes them feel heavy and uncomfortable when used for ordinary hiking.

A few companies still make leather mountaineering boots, but most of that market now belongs to plastic double boots, which have a molded plastic outer shell and a removable inner boot made of leather, vinyl, foam, or felt. Today's leather mountaineering boots are all single boots; they have no removable inner boot and very little insulation, making them suitable for

circulation, which can lead to cold feet—even frostbite.

If you're planning to carry a substantial load, try the boots on while wearing a pack. Stand on a sharp edge to test the arch support. Squat down and see if the toe box folds into a sharp wrinkle that jabs your toes. Let your foot roll to the side and check whether the boot provides adequate ankle support. You'll be surprised at how quickly a lightweight day-hiker begins to seem inadequate for serious backpacking. Unfortunately, the stiffer the boot, the harder it is to judge whether it will be comfortable over the long haul. That's another reason to buy no heavier and stiffer a boot than you really need. You're looking for summer use only. Plastic double boots, by contrast, are now the universal standard on cold, high peaks from Alaska to the Himalayas. The nonabsorbent plastic shell is a vast improvement over leather because it doesn't absorb moisture during the day, then freeze hard as iron at night.

Take extra care when fitting mountaineering boots. Leather models soften only grudgingly; the shells of plastic boots don't soften at all. With plastic boots, your only hope is that the inner boots will pack down a bit with use, allowing the foam or felt to mold comfortably to your feet. Sometimes, however, the foam compresses to the point where you'll need to wear an extra pair of socks to keep your feet from rattling around inside your boots. Heel lift (the movement of your heel up and down inside the boot) is a common problem in boots this stiff, so try to find a pair that cups your heel snugly. Whether leather or plastic, mountaineering boots sell only in limited quantities, so the price is high.

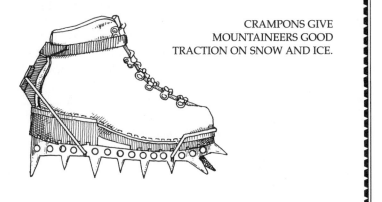

CRAMPONS GIVE MOUNTAINEERS GOOD TRACTION ON SNOW AND ICE.

the balance point between light weight and support—a balance point that will vary depending on the load on your back. Fortunately, most good shops will let you return boots within a few days after purchase if you've worn them only indoors.

BOOT CARE

Good boots are like puppies: treat them well when they're young, and they won't bite you when they're old.

The first priority is keeping your boots clean. Dirt left clinging to boots will work its way into the leather, fabric, seams, and stitching, then grind away until the boots fall apart. Consider it a moral imperative, akin to washing behind your ears, to clean your boots with water and a stiff scrub brush after a muddy trip; a little mild soap will help.

Next, dry your boots slowly, well away from any heat source. Don't put your boots any closer to a heat source than your own hand can tolerate comfortably. To speed drying, unlace the boots completely, remove the insoles (and liners if you have pac boots) and stuff the boots with dry newspaper. Replace the newspaper periodically.

Cowhide, like your skin, was naturally oily when it covered the cow. Also like your skin, cowhide can dry out, become brittle, and crack if soaked repeatedly in water or exposed continually to hot, dry conditions. Preserving leather's suppleness and waterproofness requires periodic applications of a leather conditioner. Here controversy reigns, with each manufacturer of conditioner finding some reason to claim that rival products will rot the leather, degrade the stitching, and delaminate the soles as well as give you night sweats and premature baldness. The safest course is to use the conditioner recommended by the boot manufacturer, if for no other reason than to preserve your rights under the warranty. As a general rule, manufacturers recommend silicone-based treatments such as Scotchgard and AquaSeal for silicone-impregnated leather. Other leathers used in boots, whether they are called oil-tanned, vegetable-tanned, chrome-tanned, or combination-tanned, benefit from wax-based compounds like Sno-Seal, Bee Seal Plus and Biwell. I prefer Biwell because it dries hard on the surface and therefore doesn't attract dirt. Mink oil and neat's-foot oil are intended to soften leather which has become hard and brittle; they should not be used as waterproofing agents.

Unlike puppies, boots that won't be used for a long time should be stored in a cool, dry, dark place.

PICKING A PACK THAT WORKS

"I live not in myself, but I become
Portion of that around me: and to me
High mountains are a feeling, but the hum
Of human cities torture."

—Lord Byron, *Childe Harold's Pilgrimage,* **1812**

The road to hell is paved with good packs used badly. I still wince at the thought of my own mistakes. There was the time I finished a five-day ascent of Yosemite's 3,000-vertical-foot El Capitan, then packed 60 pounds of steel and aluminum rock-climbing hardware into a day pack designed for 25-pound loads and hauled it 7 miles back down to my campsite. And the time seven friends and I climbed Alaska's 16,237-foot Mount Sanford. At the beginning of the expedition, we made two trips, carrying half our gear each time, from the bush landing strip to the foot of the glacier. Coming out, however, we were too eager for showers, pizza, and rock 'n roll to adopt such a sane approach, so we decided to make only one trip, carrying everything in one gigantic load. At the foot of the glacier, I filled my gargantuan internal-frame pack to the brim, loosened the pack lid's extension straps to their limit, crammed in some more, then lashed a fiberglass sled and heavy mountaineering skis on top. My pack must have weighed 90 pounds—about two-thirds as much as I did. I felt like an Olympic weightlifter doing the clean-and-jerk on a gold-medal weight each time I hoisted my pack. After two repetitions, it became impossible to lift it without assistance, and I was forced to ask for help in getting it on after each rest stop for the remainder of the trailless 9-mile hike out over the tundra. Fortunately, someone else agreed to carry the 12-gauge shotgun we'd brought as grizzly insurance. A couple of years later, I carried a similar-size load of camera gear into the Grand Canyon to photograph a rafting expedition. I had packed the pack while it was sitting on the tailgate of my pickup so I could slip it on without actually lifting it off the ground. That meant, however, that all the way into the canyon I could never set the pack down without finding a tailgate-high, flat-topped rock to set it on. People stopped me on the trail repeatedly and said things like, "That's the biggest pack I've ever seen." At first I was secretly proud. Then the pain got too great, and I would just smile through tight lips and keep walking.

FANNY PACKS AND DAY PACKS

If you're interested mostly in carrying an extra sweater and a water bottle during an evening jaunt or half-day stroll, then all you really need is a fanny pack or its upscale cousin with the tony name, the lumbar pack. Fanny packs range in size from watch-pocket-on-a-shoestring to breadbasket-on-a-girdle. As your hiking range increases and the weather gets more severe, you'll find the gear you need overburdening even the biggest lumbar pack. When your fanny pack starts to look like a thrift store's giveaway box, bulging at the seams and overflowing the top, it's time to move up to a day pack.

At first, you may want to carry the book pack you once used to haul *War and Peace* to school without breaking your arm. You'll quickly

A TYPICAL DAY PACK.

find, however, that you've entered a race between your growing dissatisfaction with the book pack's capacity and comfort and its accelerating tendency to explode at its flimsy zippers. I'm rooting for the zipper explosion because that will give you the perfect excuse to buy a day pack that will last you for a decade and make your hiking days a pleasure.

The day packs I like share several features. First, they pamper your shoulders with amply padded shoulder straps. Second, they protect your spine from steely-hearted, back-stabbing pieces of equipment with a foam-padded panel that covers the entire back of the pack. (Let's clarify a bit of nomenclature here: the back of your pack faces your back, while the front faces away, so you can think of yourself as a two-headed push-me pull-you as you walk down the trail.) Larger-capacity day packs, which are designed for higher loads, may protect your back with both foam padding and a sheet of stiff plastic. The plastic sheet also helps transfer weight to your hips. A well-padded hip belt makes that weight transfer more comfortable, but beware: few day packs let you adjust the height at which the pack rides relative to your waist. The wrong size day pack can leave you with a hip belt that puts the squeeze on your stomach—and that extra cheese danish you gluttonously gobbled—not your hips. I prefer day packs with simple drawstring closures at the top, referred to as top-loading packs.

The alternative is a panel-loading pack with a long U-shaped zipper arcing across the front panel. Panel-loading packs provide convenient access to all your gear, but have one serious Achilles' heel. Even the most stout zipper tends to break or wear out eventually, particularly if it's used in sandy regions. Sand and grit get into the zipper teeth, then wear out the slider from the inside. You'll start zipping your pack shut one day and find that the zipper is unzipping itself behind the slider just as fast as you zip it together in front. With many panel-loading day packs, a zipper failure leaves you with no good way to close your pack and retain the contents inside. A top-loading pack with a drawstring can't fail in this manner. Panel-loaders also have the disadvantage that they must be laid flat on their backs to access the contents—an unappealing prospect when the ground is a sea of mud, since any mud that clings to the back of the pack is transferred immediately to your clothing when you put the pack on.

Your day pack should have a few other features. Look for a large pocket in the pack lid, but be aware that it's one of Murphy's laws that you'll never have enough room in that pocket for all the essential items that you want to be accessible immediately. A flat pocket for maps, often found underneath the lid, can be convenient, but I find I never use mine, preferring instead to cram the map into the top pocket, where it's more accessible. Better day packs have compression straps

THE BEST WAY TO CARRY
SKIS IS TO SLIP THEM THROUGH
YOUR PACK'S COMPRESSION STRAPS, THEN LASH
THE TIPS TOGETHER WITH A SHORT ACCESSORY STRAP.

along the sides of the pack. These straps, usually two or three to a side, allow you to compress the load and prevent the contents from swaying to and fro, which can upset your balance when you're boulder-hopping, log-balancing, skiing or swinging through the jungle with Tarzan in hot pursuit. Compression straps also give you a convenient way to lash on extra clothing and equipment, like a fly rod, tripod, or skis. I like to slide my skis tailfirst down through the compression straps, then lash the tips together with a short strap. Lashing the tips helps keep the skis from pivoting back and forth and whacking you in the head when you walk. Be sure the tails don't drop down so low that they hook the back of your knees or catch on the ground when you're walking down a steep hill. To further simplify attaching skis, I modified the top compression strap on both sides by substituting a quick-release buckle for the normal ladder buckle, which must be rethreaded painstakingly if you undo it completely.

Most day packs provide lash patches on either the front of the pack or the lid. Lash patches are small leather or synthetic swatches of material sewn to the pack with slots behind them to accommodate lash straps, short lengths of nylon webbing with buckles on the end, used for attaching gear that won't fit inside. Technical day packs (meaning packs designed for climbers) include an ice-ax loop, a small loop of webbing at the bottom of the pack that makes attaching an ice ax convenient. Ice axes are not just for demented people who like to climb frozen waterfalls; many early-season peak-baggers carry them to stop a slip while crossing hard-frozen snowfields in the early morning. If your ambitions include such ascents, look for a day pack with an ice-ax loop. Be aware, however, that an ice ax is useless unless you know how to use it. Novice mountaineers should seek competent instruction from a qualified mountaineering school or highly experienced friends.

MULTI-DAY PACKS

Day packs have neither the capacity to accommodate the gear you'll need for an overnight trip, nor a suspension system adequate to carry the weight with reasonable comfort. As you begin shopping for a multi-day pack, you face the pack world's metaphorical Continental Divide, with external-frame packs on one side, internal-frame packs on the other.

My first multi-day pack was an external-frame Kelty with an olive-drab pack bag, purchased in the early 1970s when I was a young teen. It possessed all the virtues that external frames still have today and served me well on my first backpacking trips into the Sierras with my father. The frame itself was built of stout aluminum tubing in the form of an abbreviated ladder about 3 feet high. The two vertical members on the sides were curved to fit the curve of my spine. Four horizontal cross members provided rigidity and strength. The pack bag had one top-loading main compartment closed with a simple fabric flap and several zippered side pockets. Broad mesh bands across the back of the pack forced the pack bag to ride slightly away from my

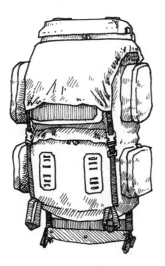

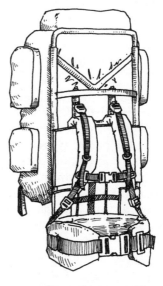

THE FRONT OF A TYPICAL EXTERNAL-FRAME PACK.

THE BACK OF A TYPICAL EXTERNAL-FRAME PACK.

back, permitting a cooling breeze to dry my sweat. The rigid frame effectively transferred most of the weight to the padded hip belt, where it belonged—your hips can carry more weight, much longer, than your shoulders. The shoulder straps served primarily to prevent the pack from toppling over backward. The forward curve of the frame as it rose above my shoulders allowed me to lash heavy items high, with the weight centered almost directly over my hips, so I could walk with a comfortable, nearly upright stance.

The same rigid frame that made carrying my Kelty so comfortable on smooth trails, however, proved to be a liability when my father and I left the trail and scrambled up a long, talus-choked couloir to the summit of Mount Agassiz, a 13,891-foot peak that provided a stunning view of the surreal turquoise blue lakes at the base of the Palisades. With the rigid frame strapped on tightly with the hip belt and shoulder straps, I felt as if I was wearing a body cast that prevented the natural bending and twisting required to keep my balance on the uneven, boulder-strewn slope. Carrying the weight high compounded the problem because it raised my center of gravity and made me top-heavy. The efficient way to travel on talus is to move rhythmically from rock to rock in a flowing dynamic balance. That goal was thwarted, however, by the pack's rigidity and high center of gravity. Similar experiences in the late 1960s led Greg Lowe to create the first parallel-stave internal-frame packs. His pioneering design is now the standard.

Lowe's goal was the first winter ascent of the north face of the Grand Teton. For that, he needed a large-capacity pack with a suspension comfortable enough to handle significant weight that would also allow him to climb effectively. His solution was a pack with two internal aluminum staves set vertically and parallel to each other in the back of the pack bag. With no horizontal cross-members to stiffen the frame, the pack could flex enough to permit a long reach for a good hold or a graceful jump turn while skiing steep snow. The staves were bent to fit the natural curve of the back, so the weight rode very close to the body, reducing the top-heavy feeling of carrying an external frame and preventing the pack bag from swaying to and fro and throwing the climber or skier off-balance. Other pack makers jumped on the bandwagon, and soon internal-frame packs were the standard for mountaineers, backcountry skiers, and an increasing number of backpackers as well. I bought my first internal-frame pack in 1978, shortly before my first expedition to Alaska, and I've been using them almost exclusively ever since.

Internal frames do have disadvantages. The back of your shirt is guaranteed to be soaked with sweat after an hour or two of walking because no cooling breeze can force itself into the paper-thin gap between your pack and your back. The load typically rides lower than in

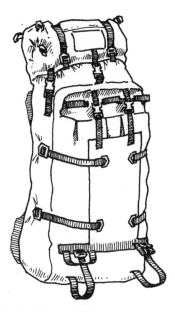 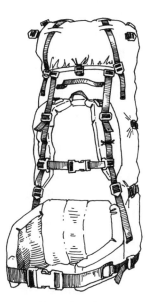

THE FRONT OF A TYPICAL INTERNAL-
FRAME PACK.

THE BACK OF A TYPICAL INTERNAL-
FRAME PACK.

an external frame, which is good for balance but more tiring, because it enforces a vaguely simian forward-leaning posture. Internal frames are also less forgiving of packing errors, such as stowing the heaviest items at the bottom, and they're usually more expensive as well. (I'll discuss packing later, in more detail.)

If you plan to stick mostly to moderately rough summer trails, particularly if you think you'll be carrying massive loads, consider a frame pack. If winter snowshoe or ski trips or lots of off-trail scrambling are in your plans, then an internal frame is a better bet. External frames have one other virtue: they make it easy to carry heavy, awkwardly shaped loads, like big tripods, that don't fit easily into an internal frame.

AIR TRAVEL

Backpackers who travel frequently by air put additional demands on their packs. Airport baggage workers have impeccable records when it comes to handling packs—they've never yet let one through unscarred. External frames sometimes get bent or broken; airport conveyor belts occasionally shear off a few of the straps and buckles that adorn internal frames. If you must send your pack on an airplane unprotected by a steel case, try to snug down all the straps and tuck the ends inside, or tie them together to reduce the length and number of loose ends. A better solution is to wrap your pack, of either type, with a foam sleeping pad, then throw the entire mummified affair into a giant duffel bag. Just don't use your Therm-A-Rest or, even worse, your $500 Gore-Tex down sleeping bag as padding. Another solution, which dispenses with the need to carry or store a duffel bag once you arrive, is to buy a specialized travel pack.

Travel packs, all of which have internal frames, allow you to hide the suspension behind a fabric panel or to remove the suspension completely. At one end of the spectrum, travel packs can be glorified suitcases with uncomfortably skimpy shoulder straps. You wouldn't want to carry one on your back farther than the VIP slots of a small parking lot. At the spectrum's other end are full-featured packs suitable for week-long treks. Despite pack makers' best efforts, however, even sophisticated travel packs tend to be a compromise between carrying comfort on the trail and durability while traveling. My preference is to protect my expedition-grade pack with a big duffel bag when I travel by air.

Be sure to take these additional precautions before heading to the airport. First, make sure that your pack/duffel bag combo doesn't exceed the weight limit for a single piece of luggage. Excess baggage charges add up very fast: 70 pounds is the limit on most domestic flights. Limits on small planes and overseas flights may be less, depending on the carrier. Some duffel bags and packs have double-pull zippers, with two adjacent sliders that let you unzip the bag from either end. Consider locking those two zipper pulls together to discourage casual theft. Don't bring any backpacking fuel on board, whether in your stove, in your fuel bottle or in the form of butane cartridges, whether attached to your stove or not. Carrying fuel on board is illegal because it creates a severe fire hazard. After emptying your stove and fuel bottle, triple bag them to prevent fumes from contaminating clothing or food. One plastic bag won't necessarily stop all odors from penetrating your goodies. Bill Baker and I learned this the hard way during a nine-day, 150-mile sea-kayak journey in Kenai Fjords National Park. Bill had just purchased two brand-new fiberglass kayaks. Two days out, we discovered that the pilot crackers we'd brought as a mainstay were absorbing fiberglass odors right through the heavy plastic bags in which we'd stored them.

SELECTING AND FITTING A MULTI-DAY PACK

Treated with care, a well-built pack will last for years. After a decade of hard use, I'm still carrying the second day pack I've owned. The first one, a gift from my father over twenty years ago, would probably still be going strong if I hadn't destroyed it hauling it up granite rock-climbs in Yosemite and Rocky Mountain National Park. Right now I'm using my fifth multi-day pack. None of the four previous packs ever really wore out. I just decided that the grass would be greener if I jumped over the fence and bought that shiny new red pack with the come-hither gleam in its eye. The durability of a good pack makes it important to choose carefully. Take the time, and spend the money, to get a pack you think you'll be happy with for years.

The way a pack fits is the overriding criterion. However, finding such a pack is not quite as simple as it might seem.

In 1983 I guided an expedition on Mount McKinley. My assistant, Janet Gelman, was a former college ski racer who had once broken her back in a skiing accident. One week into the three-week expedition, her old injury began to hurt again. She was carrying a nearly-new, top-quality internal-frame pack almost identical to the one I was carrying in relative comfort. (I say "relative" because carrying 60 pounds for eight hours will make your shoulders sore no matter what pack you're carrying.) Like most women, she had a much shorter torso than the average male. Like most packs, hers had been designed for the average male torso. The result was a pack that always rode too low on her hips and put too much strain on her back, no matter how she adjusted it. Finally, in desperation, she took a stout sewing awl called a Speedy Stitcher and modified the suspension of her pack so it would ride higher on her back—a painstaking operation that took several numb-fingered hours at 14,300 feet.

The moral of this story may seem obvious: make sure your pack fits before you buy it. However, as my assistant found out, and as I've experienced myself with other packs, it can take a week or two of use, combined with constant fiddling, to get a pack's suspension tweaked to perfection. When buying a pack, look for a suspension that is as adjustable as possible. If you can, select a pack that seems to fit best when using the middle portion of the adjustment range, giving you the option of altering the fit in either direction.

Trying on an empty pack tells you nothing about the fit, so most good outdoor shops keep sandbags of varying weights in the pack department. Toss 25 or 30 pounds into the pack you're considering, then walk around the shop for a few minutes. You'll quickly gain a much better feel for the pack's load-carrying comfort. Women who find that men's packs don't fit should seek out a pack from one of the companies that now make packs specifically for women. However, even these provide no guarantee of a perfect fit. The hip belt on Cora's first internal-frame pack, although designed specifically for women, was too long to cinch snugly about her small hips. We had to shorten the belt with a Speedy Stitcher to make it comfortable for her.

Internal- and external-frame packs share similarities in the way they're fitted, even if the mechanism for making alterations is quite different. The first and most important adjustment is the distance between the hip belt and the point where the upper end of the shoulder straps attaches to the frame or pack bag. Let's call this the pack's torso-length adjustment. If this distance is too short, the pack's hip belt will ride too high, encircling your stomach instead of your hips when the shoulder straps are adjusted properly. If this distance is too long, the hip belt will ride too low, even if you tighten the shoulder straps as far as they will go. A low-rider hip belt, chic though it may appear, will constrict the muscles in your buttocks and the outside of your hips, causing discomfort and fatigue, and potentially causing back pain. This is the problem my assistant guide experienced on McKinley. If the torso-length adjustment is set correctly, the hip belt will cradle the tops of your hipbones, and most of the pack's weight will ride comfortably on your hips. Normally, you'll only need to adjust the torso length once during the life of the pack. With the torso length correct, all the other adjustments should fall into place easily.

Sophisticated external-frame packs allow you to adjust the torso length by moving the attachment points of both the shoulder straps and the hip belt. On less expensive frame packs, the upper end of the shoulder straps attaches directly to a fixed horizontal frame member, so the height of the shoulder-strap attachment cannot be adjusted. Some of these inexpensive frame packs allow you to adjust the height of the hip belt's attachment to the frame; others provide different frame sizes to fit different torso lengths. The least expensive frame packs come in one size. Avoid these unless you're positive they fit perfectly and your primary concern is saving money.

To determine whether the torso length you've selected for an external-frame pack is correct, first load the pack and slip it on. Adjust the shoulder straps to approximately the right fit, neither so tight that they squeeze your shoulders uncomfortably, nor so loose that the pack seems to be dragging you over backward. Then fasten the hip belt and cinch it down firmly. It should snugly cup the high points of your pelvis. The pack's weight should feel as though it's riding mostly on your hips. Now, if need be, tighten the shoulder straps slightly. The shoulder straps should be horizontal where they attach to the pack frame. In other words, the attachment point should be the same height as the top of your shoulders. If necessary, adjust the torso length until both hip belt and shoulder straps fit correctly. Once you have the torso length correct, check a few other points. Are the shoulder straps acting like vampires, drawing blood from your neck because they're too close together? Are they so far apart that they weight the outermost parts of your shoulders uncomfortably? Good packs let you adjust the distance between the shoulder straps to fit your anatomy.

Internal-frame packs use a different method to adjust the torso length. With most internal frames, the upper end of the shoulder straps attaches to the shoulder yoke, which is positioned approximately between your shoulder blades. The height of this shoulder yoke can be adjusted up or down, usually via some arrangement of straps and buckles. Regardless of the method, the goal is the same as with an external-frame pack: proper positioning of the shoulder straps in relation to the hip belt so that the pack's weight rides primarily on your hips, with the shoulder straps serving mostly to prevent the pack from swaying dramatically from side to side or falling over backward.

The advantage of attaching the shoulder straps to a shoulder yoke is that the straps wrap more comfortably around your shoulders than they do with an external frame. The disadvantage of the shoulder-yoke design is the greater potential for the pack to sway. To prevent swaying, and to further reduce the pressure on your shoulders, internal-frame packs have shoulder-stabilizer straps, also known as load-lifter straps. These straps attach to the shoulder straps at about your clavicle, then extend upward at a 45° angle to the pack's aluminum staves. Snug down your shoulder-stabilizer straps, then loosen the shoulder straps a bit, and the result is almost magical relief for your aching shoulders as the load shifts even more completely to your hip belt. When your hips start to complain, tighten the shoulder straps again, loosen the shoulder-stabilizers a little, and shift some weight back to your shoulders. These adjustments can be made on the trail, almost without breaking stride. Only the best external-frame packs offer shoulder-stabilizer straps.

Good internal frames can be fine-tuned even further. In an effort to allow your hips to move independently of your shoulders, the hip belt on most internal frames fastens to a lumbar pad that rides in the small of your back. By moving the attachment points of the hip belt relatively close to each other, rather than positioning them at the out side corners of the pack bag, your hips can rock up and down like a teeter-totter when you walk without pushing the pack bag up and down at the same time. That reduces fatigue and increases comfort, but introduces the possibility that your pack could roll side to side like a barrel on your back. To reduce that motion, pack designers introduced hip-stabilizer straps that run from the bottom corners of the pack bag to the hip belt. These work great unless your name is Elvis. They should be loosened each time you remove your pack, then tightened again after you've put on your pack and snugged down your hip belt.

The final adjustment—almost universal now on internal frames and increasingly common on external frames—involves the sternum strap, which connects the shoulder straps at the level of your breastbone. This strap lets you fine tune where the shoulder straps ride on your shoulders. The attachment points of the sternum straps to the shoulder straps can usually be adjusted up or down so the sternum strap rides in a comfortable place.

By now you may feel that buying a modern pack means you'll spend half your vacation reading instructions and yanking on puzzling pieces of webbing rather than enjoying the wilderness. Perhaps pack makers are actually engaged in a diabolical plot to keep befuddled novices near the trail head so they won't overcrowd the pack makers' favorite wilderness valleys. With a little perseverance, however, you can master your pack's intricacies, defeat this sinister scheme, and stride forth confidently into the wilds. Whatever you may read in the instructions, no matter whether you're carrying an external frame or an internal frame, your comfort is the final arbiter. Keep tweaking that suspension until it feels right, even if it means stopping in the middle of the hike to fiddle with it. Preventive maintenance on your pack's suspension will repay you many times over.

Like day packs, the pack bags that accompany both external- and internal-frame packs come in two basic styles: top-loading, in which you stuff everything in the top while holding the pack upright, and panel-loading, in which you lay the pack flat on its back and unzip a large panel on the pack's front. Simple top-loading internal frames close with a single drawstring. More complex internal frames have, in addition, a spindrift collar; essentially an extension of the main pack body that closes over the contents when the pack is full to keep blowing snow from sneaking into the pack. The pack lid on an internal frame with a spindrift collar often "floats." Adjustable straps allow the lid to be raised to cover an overstuffed pack, or be lowered to cover the pack's opening when the load is smaller. Floating lids and spindrift collars are particularly useful to winter campers, long-distance trekkers and people who backpack with kids, all of whom need room for large volumes of clothing and food. Although in public I espouse the gospel of going fast and light, I'm actually a closet believer in comfort in camp. I'm also a photo-fanatic who can't resist bringing a massive Nikon camera body, multiple lenses, a flash, flash meter and tripod, plus the clothing necessary to remain comfortable during a subfreezing sunrise shoot at timberline. I use the full capacity of my internal-frame, floating-lid load-monster embarrassingly often, even on overnight weekend trips.

Most external-frame packs, whether top-loading or panel-loading, have a light aluminum framework called the hold-open bar at the top of the pack bag. On a top-loading pack, the hold-open bar keeps the mouth of the bag open for easy loading. On a panel-loader, it provides structure to the pack bag when the front panel is zipped open, again making loading easier. Large-capacity external frames often have a frame extension that rises above the hold-open bar. The extension provides additional lashing points when your gear begins multiplying like a family of love-starved guppies.

In general, I prefer top-loading packs, whether internal frame or external frame, because they have no zippers to blow out and because you don't have to lay the suspension side flat in the mud to get at the contents. The disadvantage of a top-loader, particularly one with a single undivided compartment, is that you have to think carefully about what goes in first, because everything else will go in on top, burying the items on the bottom and making them inconvenient to get at when you're on the trail. The solution, of course, is to put items you won't need during the day, like your tent, sleeping bag and stove, at the bottom. The problem of accessibility is manageable, but some people still prefer panel-loaders because they provide easy access to all of their gear at any time.

Pack bags for both internal and external frames are normally made of pack cloth, a tough nylon weighing about 8 ounces per square yard that easily is durable enough for normal use. Often a second layer of pack cloth or a tougher material called Cordura is used to reinforce the bottom of internal-frame pack bags. A few packs are made entirely of Cordura. This is overkill unless you're planning to drag your pack up the south face of Everest.

If you choose an internal-frame, you'll need a pack with a capacity of 3,000 to 4,500 cubic inches for trips of two to three days. A capacity of 4,500 to 6,000 cubic inches should work well for a week-long trek. Anything over 6,000 is for a full-blown Alaskan or Himalayan expedition. The capacity of an external frame's pack bag can be 1,500 or 2,000 cubic inches smaller because it's assumed that you'll be lashing your sleeping bag and tent to the frame above and below the pack bag. A good way to add convenience and a little extra capacity to an internal-frame pack is buy the accessory side pockets that many manufacturers offer. These usually attach to the compression straps on the side of the pack. Side pockets do make you a bit more broad of beam, which is a disadvantage when canyoneering and bushwhacking.

THE TENTS DECISION: CHOOSING A WILDERNESS SHELTER

"How hard to realize that every camp of men or beast has this glorious starry firmament for a roof! In such places standing alone on the mountaintop it is easy to realize that whatever special nests we make—leaves and moss like the marmots and birds, or tents or piled stone—we all dwell in a house of one room—the world with the firmament for its roof—and are sailing the celestial spaces without leaving any track."

—John Muir, *John of the Mountains*, 1938

As a teenager venturing forth on my first backpacking trips, I was inspired by the example of John Muir, who roamed the High Sierra in the 1870s for days on end, burdened only by a greatcoat, its pockets stuffed with biscuits. The ponderous sleeping bags and tents of his day were more suited to carting on the back of a mule than on the bowed shoulders of a human being, and Muir rightly preferred to ramble unencumbered. My attempts to emulate his example, however, soon showed me just how miserable such spartan camping can be.

In August, 1979, two friends and I set out to climb Mount Fay in the Canadian Rockies. We started up the approach in the evening, then bivouacked near the base of a steep, ice-floored gully with crumbling rock walls. Our plan was to rise before dawn and complete the ascent of the gully before the morning sun thawed the ice holding the shattered gully walls together and turned the gully into a bowling alley with 50-pound limestone blocks as bowling balls and ourselves as human bowling pins. With no tent or sleeping bags, we would be traveling light and fast in the best tradition of John Muir.

The problem, as we quickly discovered, was that our bodies needed far more insulation to remain comfortable while sleeping than we expected. We donned every scrap of clothing we'd brought and curled ourselves into the tightest little balls we could, and still we were shivering and squirming. The idea of carrying an extra five or six pounds of sleeping gear, which we had scorned just hours before, suddenly seemed irresistible. "You have to spend at least part of each year living this way," said Joe Kaelin, rolling over for the twentieth time in a futile effort to rewarm those body parts which were nearing frostbite through contact with the cold ground. As I vowed never again to spend a night outdoors without at least a sleeping bag, I wondered whether Joe had succumbed to the notion that self-denial would lead to mystic revelations, or whether his ambitions extended only to enshrinement in the pantheon of climbing heroes. We rose long before dawn—no need for an alarm clock; we were all wide awake—and climbed the gully as fast as our sleep-starved bodies would allow us. At mid-morning we reached the high mountain hut that sat on the plateau above the gully and promptly took a long nap. After a much more comfortable night in the hut, we climbed Mount Fay the next day.

Muir may well have been much tougher than we were; he was certainly a mystic who verged on asceticism at times. However, he also availed himself freely, I suspect, of a luxury no longer available to the outdoorsmen of today: a crackling fire, perhaps built so its warmth would reflect off a granite boulder onto his backside. Fortunately, modern tents and sleeping bags make it easy to camp in comfort using only the gear you can readily carry on your back, while the burgeoning hordes of wilderness enthusiasts make fire-building reprehensible in most situations. (I'll have more to say about campfires in Chapter 11.)

CAMPING WITHOUT A TENT

Today very few backpackers venture into the wilderness without a sleeping bag. A few still insist, however, that a full-fledged tent is an unnecessary burden, at least in some situations. In my young and impoverished days, I sometimes used a tube tent, a 10-foot-long, 5-foot-diameter tube of polyethylene. A string running through the tube and tied between two trees at chest height held the tube erect in the form of a poor man's pup tent. The disadvantages of a tube tent soon became apparent: rainwater flowing along the ground quickly entered the high end of the wide-open tube, then obstinately pooled inside, while mosquitoes circulated in and out freely, each obtaining their pint of blood en route.

The other alternatives to a full-on tent are scarcely an improvement over the tube tent. Some backpackers still use a simple tarp, measuring about 9 by 12 feet in size, erected with the aid of guy lines and tree trunks. However, the same objections apply. In desert regions where rain is a rarity, a few hardy campers advocate the "Visqueen burrito." Spread your sleeping bag out on a plastic ground sheet (Visqueen is one trade name) and hope you won't be rudely awakened by fat raindrops exploding on your face. If you're unlucky, pretend you've just become a gooey mass of beans and cheese and roll yourself up in the ground sheet as if it was a tortilla. If the rainstorm is brief, the Visqueen burrito trick can work well and save you considerable weight. If you remain wrapped in your plastic tortilla all night, however, you'll be a very soggy burrito come morning. Condensation inside the impermeable plastic will have soaked your sleeping bag. The high-tech version of the Visqueen burrito is the bivouac sack, a waterproof bag a little bigger than a sleeping bag that is usually made of Gore-Tex. Bivouac sacks are the favored overnight shelter of alpinists intent on difficult multi-day ascents of routes in moderate climates, but they're too small to do anything in them but sleep. The only backpackers who use them are extremely weight-conscious types not faced with the possibility of waiting out a three-day blow.

Enlightened by my early experiences with tube tents, I became forever skeptical of any wilderness shelter short of a full-fledged tent. The addition of a few extra pounds to the pack in the form of a tent makes the whole trip more enjoyable. The southwestern deserts can be an exception, as they are bug- and rain-free in most seasons. Camping under the stars there can be a delight. But for all mountain trips, in any season, I bring a tent.

BASIC TENT DESIGNS

Once upon a time, in the days when all tent poles were as straight and rigid as a drill sergeant's spine, the A-frame or pup tent was the standard American backcountry tent. A-frames usually have two poles at each end in the form of an inverted V, plus a ridge pole forming the tent's backbone. While similar tents have been used for thousands of years, A-frames suffer from several inherent disadvantages. First, the broad, flat areas of unsupported fabric provide a perfect target for the wind, which sets the fabric to flapping loudly like a

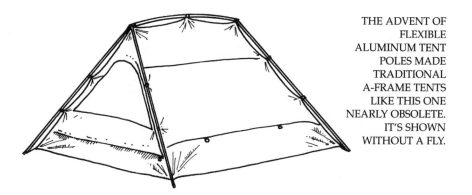

THE ADVENT OF FLEXIBLE ALUMINUM TENT POLES MADE TRADITIONAL A-FRAME TENTS LIKE THIS ONE NEARLY OBSOLETE. IT'S SHOWN WITHOUT A FLY.

flag in a hurricane, robbing the beleaguered occupants of sleep. Second, the design uses materials inefficiently. Usable interior space is small in relation to the tent's weight, since the uniformly sloping walls restrict the occupants' ability to sit up anywhere but the middle of the tent. Finally, pitching an A-frame properly usually requires many stakes and guy lines, which are guaranteed to trip you up when you stagger groggily out of the tent at 2:00 A.M. to relieve yourself.

Like A-frames, pyramid tents reigned in the days when the only available tent poles were straight. As the name implies, pyramids resemble a miniaturized version of some pharaoh's monument to his ego, with a single central pole supporting the tent's peak. The same disadvantages that have relegated A-frames to the dustbin of tent design have forced retirement onto the pyramid, with one exception: a few pyramidal-shaped, floorless tarps supported by a single central pole can still be seen occasionally.

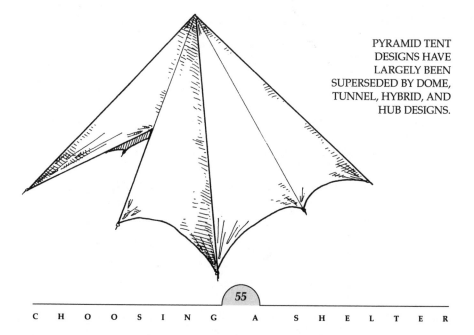

PYRAMID TENT DESIGNS HAVE LARGELY BEEN SUPERSEDED BY DOME, TUNNEL, HYBRID, AND HUB DESIGNS.

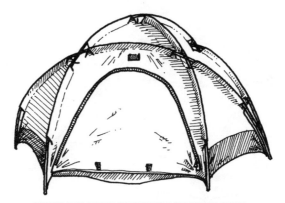

FOUR-POLE DOME TENTS LIKE THIS ONE,
SHOWN WITHOUT A FLY, ARE VERY STRONG
AND ARE OFTEN USED IN THE WINTER.

The invention of strong, flexible aluminum poles set tent designers loose on an orgy of innovation that still hasn't stopped. Dome tents, shaped like a hemisphere, offer the greatest interior volume of any tent for a given surface area of tent fabric, which gives them a good volume-to-weight ratio. The tent walls are almost vertical near the ground, so occupants can sit up anywhere in the tent, greatly increasing the usable amount of floor space compared to an A-frame or pyramid. Geodesic domes, or geodomes, are supported by an interlocking structure of three or four poles that intersect to form triangles. This design means that only small areas of fabric are unsupported by poles. Dome tents easily shrug off high winds and resist the weight of accumulating snow. Most winter and expedition tents are geodomes. All domes are freestanding, which means that they don't need to be staked in order to stand upright; however, all *must* be staked to prevent them from taking

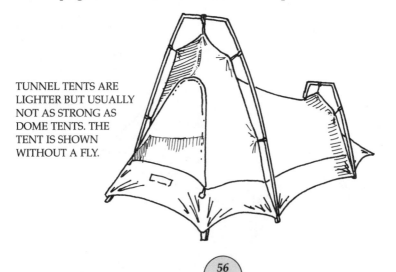

TUNNEL TENTS ARE
LIGHTER BUT USUALLY
NOT AS STRONG AS
DOME TENTS. THE
TENT IS SHOWN
WITHOUT A FLY.

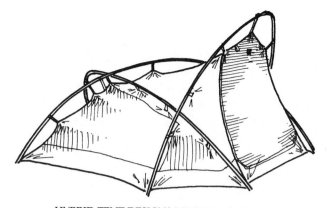

HYBRID TENT DESIGNS LIKE THIS ONE,
SHOWN WITHOUT A FLY, LET TENT
DESIGNERS CREATE FUNCTIONAL
SCULPTURES IN FABRIC.

off like a kite when the breeze blows. When empty, freestanding tents can be picked up and moved without disassembling them, a convenient feature if the first site you pick proves to be an ant hill.

Tunnel tents or hoop tents, shaped like a half-cylinder, run a close second to dome tents in their volume-to-surface-area measurements. They often use fewer poles than domes, which gives them larger areas of unsupported fabric, but saves weight. Designers have also experimented with nearly every other possible design using continuous-arc poles, producing a wide variety of hybrids that fall somewhere between the basic dome and tunnel shapes. Many tents intended for summer use employ tunnel or hybrid designs.

In recent years, yet another variation has debuted: hub tents, in which flexible poles radiate from one or more molded plastic hubs located along the tent's spine. The pole structure gives some hub tents

HUB TENTS CAN BE A
BIT LIGHTER THAN
DOME TENTS BECAUSE
NOT ALL POLES MUST
TERMINATE AT THE
GROUND; SOME CAN
TERMINATE AT A HUB,
SAVING THE WEIGHT
OF THE EXTRA LENGTH
OF POLE. THIS TENT IS
SHOWN WITHOUT A
FLY.

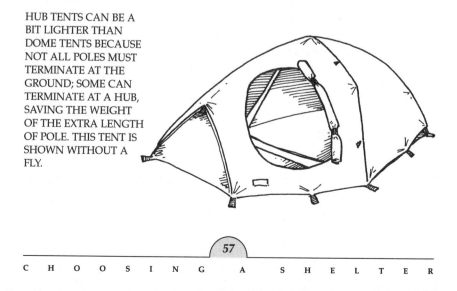

the look of sinister sci-fi insects; one designer named his creation the Preying Mantis. The principal advantage claimed for hub designs is that the poles cannot move in relation to each other where they intersect, since they're connected via a rigid hub. This increases the tent's rigidity and therefore its ability to resist wind and shed snow. Hub designs can also be lighter, since not all poles have to reach to the ground; instead, they can terminate at a hub. In most hub designs, the poles remain attached to the hub at one end with elastic shock cord. Theoretically, at least, this can simplify pitching.

CONDENSATION

Condensation in tents has bedeviled designers ever since Julius Caesar set out to conquer Gaul. Condensation occurs when warm, moist air encounters a cooler surface and is cooled below the dew point, the temperature at which the air is saturated with moisture and dew begins to form. In a tent, your breath is the most common (and unavoidable) source of warm, moist air. A person can exhale a pint of moisture per night. Evaporation of sweat and moisture from rain-soaked clothing further humidifies the air and increases the threat of condensation. Cooking inside a tent adds still more water vapor to the air, but that's by far the least of your worries. Running a stove in a poorly ventilated tent poses an extreme danger of poisoning by carbon monoxide. Cooking in any tent—even with the door and windows wide open—creates a serious fire hazard and should be avoided.

Nearly all tents sold today fight condensation with a double-walled design that uses a waterproof rain fly over a nonwaterproof tent body, called the canopy. In theory, warm, moist air will rise through the uncoated canopy and condense on the fly. In temperatures above freezing, it will then roll down the inside of the fly and drip onto the ground, instead of on the occupants. In temperatures below freezing, the moisture will congeal into frost. If the wind shakes off the frost, it will land on the canopy and slide harmlessly down to the ground. The theory works, in most conditions, although you then have to deal with a wet or frosty rain fly in the morning. Be sure that any tent you're considering provides a good separation between the fly and canopy. If they touch, either when the tent is buffeted by the wind, or when you brush up against the tent wall, condensation on the fly is sure to penetrate the canopy.

In severe cold, as well as in certain other conditions of cool temperatures and high humidity, the canopy's temperature can be below the dew point, so that moisture condenses on the canopy instead of passing through to the fly. I still remember waking up at 17,200 feet on McKinley to find a veritable snowstorm raging inside the tent. Moisture from three deep-breathing bodies had condensed to a thick frost on the canopy. As the tent trembled under assault by the ever-present wind, the frost sifted down and covered everything. Opening our tightly closed sleeping-bag hoods even a crack permitted a cascade of ice crystals to pour onto our faces. The only solution was to use the whisk broom we'd brought for just this purpose to dust off our sleeping bags and gear, then sweep the floor and shovel the piles of frost crystals out the door.

Tent makers also try to prevent condensation by providing ventilation in various ways. The problem is providing a way to let warm air escape without permitting rain to enter. Vents that penetrate the canopy but not the fly do little good. Opening the door can help if the fly extends as an awning over the door to prevent the entry of rain. Opening doors or windows on opposite sides of the tent (if the tent is so equipped) permits cross-ventilation, which works well if the night is graced by a breeze. The best venting system combines roof-level and floor-level vents, so that warm, rising air can naturally flow out the top vent while cooler air flows in the bottom. Very few tents have a high/low venting system, however, because such vents are hard to seal against rain.

One group of tents that do have such a vent system is made by Stephenson Warmlite Equipment of Gilford, New Hampshire. Stephenson tents are unusual in another way: both walls of his double-walled tents are made of waterproof material. The idea is to prevent condensation by keeping the inner wall warmer than the dew point. Stephenson tents try to achieve that by capitalizing on the "storm-window effect," in which two panes of glass (or tent fabric) trap still air between them. That still air acts as an insulator, keeping the inner layer of fabric warm. To further increase the temperature of the inner layer, Stephenson uses an aluminized fabric that acts as a radiant-heat barrier. I've used Stephenson tents on three expeditions to the Alaska Range and found that they keep condensation to a minimum. One final virtue: Stephenson tents use prebent, large-diameter poles that are some four times as strong as the typical flexible aluminum poles found in most other tents, yet are exceedingly light. The two-person Stephenson 2R tent weighs just 3 pounds, 4 ounces. On the negative side, the tents are expensive, and the lightweight coating on the ultralight fabric will wear through more quickly than heavier coatings, requiring more frequent touch-up with seam sealant.

The other maverick in the tent business is Todd Bibler, a mountaineer turned paraglider-pilot whose company makes single-walled tents out of ToddTex—essentially, Gore-Tex by another name. Until 1986, W. L. Gore made a Gore-Tex tent fabric that several manufacturers used in a variety of tents. Unfortunately, those tents could not pass the rather arbitrary fire-retardancy tests that conventional tents could, and so could not be sold in a handful of states. Eventually, Gore took the fabric off the market. Most tent manufacturers abandoned any attempt to make tents of waterproof/breathable material, but not Bibler, who found a way to produce his own version of Gore's tent fabric. Bibler tents are well made and very lightweight, but are quite expensive. In my limited experience with them, the fabric seemed to breathe well, and condensation was minimal.

CHOOSING A TENT

Which tent design is best for you? It depends on when and where you want to camp, how much weight you're willing to carry, and how much you're willing to spend. Three-season tents, designed for spring, summer and fall, typically try to save weight by using tunnel, hybrid, or hub designs that require only two or three poles. However, these lightweight tents start to whimper and whine when the wind cranks up, and they knuckle under quickly when menaced by a bully of a snowstorm. Weights for good-quality three-season tents range from just over 3 to over 7 pounds. Floor areas in the two-person models run from under 30 square feet, which is adequate but snug, up to a spacious 45 square feet. Larger tents, naturally, are more comfortable in camp, but the extra weight means longer and harder hours on the trail. Which size tent is right for you depends, in part, on your backpacking style. Do you like to hike in a short distance, set up a base camp, and day-hike from there? Or do you prefer to move camp every day and cover lots of miles?

Many three-season tents have canopies made largely of mosquito netting. When the weather is fair, you can remove the fly and enjoy every cooling breeze while gloating over the frustration of the mosquitoes pressing their hungry little noses up against the netting. In winter, however, these tents are cold, and spindrift kicked up by the wind and blown up under the fly tends to sift down on the occupants—two more reasons that netting-canopy tents are intended only for three-season use. A vestibule—an extension of the rain fly over the ground in front of the door, like an awning on a porch—is particularly valuable in rainy weather because it provides a relatively dry place to cook and store some gear.

Four-season tents, which are really designed primarily for one season—winter—are primarily domes that use four or even five interlocking poles that provide a great deal of strength and rigidity at the cost of greater weight, which varies from 7 to 10 pounds. Floor areas for two-person models range from 45 to 55 square feet (including the vestibule) to provide extra room for bulky winter gear and to help prevent tent fever. Long, cold, winter nights force winter campers to spend far more hours inside their tents than summer campers do. In winter, the subtleties of tent design become more important. For example, you should be able to pitch a good winter tent without removing your gloves. Avoid tents with a flat spot at the apex of the roof, which will collect snow. Doors set into a sloping wall also tend to collect snow, which must be knocked off before the door is opened, or else snow will fall into the tent. Doors set into vertical walls—particularly if the door opens from the top down—create fewer problems. Don't assume that any backpacking tent you buy, whether rated four-season or not, will stand up to everything. Tents that will take the worst possible winds are described more aptly as buildings. The tent that famed British explorer Eric Shipton used while sledging across the Patagonian ice cap weighed 50 pounds. The Whillans Box that some expeditions laboriously hauled to their high camp on Everest weighed 30 pounds. If a tent is light enough to be carried readily on your back, there is a gale out there, somewhere, that can destroy it.

Whether you're looking at a four-season or a three-season tent, the majority of high-quality tent poles today are made of aluminum. Fiberglass poles are generally weaker, heavier and less expensive, but a few exceptions exist. Other signs of quality include tight, even stitching, with no fabric puckers that can concentrate stresses and create starting points for tears. The rain fly should generously overlap the coated portion of the canopy walls. Good tents also have a tub floor, in which the seams that join the floor to the sidewalls are raised off the ground by the design of the tent. Seams are always potential leak points, and the fewer seams in contact with wet ground, the better. If at all possible, pitch the tent you're considering at the store before buying it. A good tent should set up easily and be as tight as your belly after Thanksgiving dinner. Slack fabric will flap in the wind and drive you nuts. Climb inside with a friend and try to imagine living in the tent during a prolonged storm. If you start contemplating murder-by-tent-peg after five minutes, buy a bigger tent.

CARING FOR YOUR TENT

Good tents are expensive, but they will give you many years of service if you take the time to care for them properly. Before using your tent for the first time, seal the seams with one of the products available in backpacking shops, then reapply sealant as needed. Seam sealing is like paying taxes: it's funny how quickly the time passes before duty calls again. Let the sealant dry thoroughly before packing away the tent. Uncured sealant is an effective glue. A few of the more expensive tents now are sold with factory-sealed seams, which is a great convenience.

Do your best to keep your tent clean. Don't wear dirty, muddy boots inside; the grit will grind away at the coating. After each night's

camp, shake all the loose sand and dirt out of the tent before stuffing it back into its stuff sack. Pay particular attention to keeping the zippers clean. Zippers are fragile under the best of circumstances, and dirty zippers wear out faster. The first item to fail on your tent is likely to be a zipper. Tent floors are punctured more easily than you might think. During the expedition to McKinley that I guided in 1983, my assistant kicked her heel on the tent floor, trying to force her feet into her stiff, heavy mountaineering boots. She put her heel right through the floor. Sharp rocks and sticks can also cause tears if you pitch your tent atop them. A little ripstop repair tape, available at most backpacking shops, can patch small tears until you can get home and repair the tent permanently.

Avoid scraping the protective coating off aluminum poles. The coating is important to prevent corrosion, which can lead to the sudden failure of the poles through a phenomenon called stress-corrosion cracking. Keep the pole joints clean, so they don't jam together. When assembling a folded bundle of pole segments, don't hold onto the last segment and flip the bundle of segments forward, letting the pole assemble itself through the action of the elastic shock cord. This tactic is guaranteed to get dirt in the joints and allow the pole-segment ends to nick each other, causing the shock cord to fray. Instead, assemble the pole segments by hand, one by one, making sure each joint is clean. When you get home, pitch the tent in your backyard, if the weather's dry, or in a spare bedroom or garage, if it's raining. Gently sponge off any mud or dirt, and let the tent dry thoroughly. Storing a tent wet will cause the coating to mildew and peel like sunburned skin. Maintaining a tent is like nailing down the loose shingles on your roof: it reduces the chance that you'll wake up one night to the ominous drip, drip, drip that spells trouble.

SLEEPING BAGS

> "On the mountains there is freedom! The world is perfect everywhere, save where man comes with his torment."
>
> —Johann Christoph Friedrich von Schiller, *The Bride of Messina*, 1803

In July 1978, when I embarked on my first expedition to the Alaska Range, nearly all mountaineers used sleeping bags filled with down, the fluffy underfeathers of ducks and geese. By comparison, sleeping bags filled with the synthetic alternatives of the day were quite heavy and bulky for the warmth they offered. However, synthetics did offer one advantage, which became apparent soon after a bush pilot deposited our four-man team on the Ruth Glacier near Mount Huntington.

The day after we landed, the sun vanished and a week-long onslaught of wet snow and rain began. Despite good rain gear and our best efforts, we gradually got wet. The inside of the tents became damp, then soggy, then positively swampy. Inevitably, our sleeping bags became soaked. The three owners of down bags saw the loft of their bags shrink every day, until the bags became frigid sheets of nylon enclosing saturated feathers. I still have a photograph of Angus Thuermer wringing water out of his worthless down bag. Joe Kaelin's synthetic bag, on the other hand, retained its loft and, therefore, a bit more of its warmth. When the sun finally did return, Joe's bag dried much faster than our down ones. The moral is simple: if you let your down bag get wet, it will become just a watered-down version of its former self.

As this anecdote shows, the climate where you'll be backpacking helps determine whether a synthetic or down-filled bag is best for you. Despite the fiasco with the down bag I carried on Mount Huntington, I've brought a down bag on every subsequent trip to the Alaska Range. Why? Because all of my other trips were to much higher—and therefore colder—peaks, where rain never falls and where keeping a down bag dry was much easier than it was on Huntington.

In some ways, choosing a sleeping bag is more difficult than selecting a pack or tent, where every feature is exposed to view. With a sleeping bag, however, you can see only the inner and outer portions of the shell, leading to the crucial question: what is really inside this thing? Your best defense is a good offense: go to a well-established specialty outdoor shop which stakes its reputation on providing quality products. Discount-store bags are for carrying on the backs of vehicles; they're too ponderous to tote on your back.

THE UPS OF DOWN

Your first task is choosing the filling. High-quality down still provides more warmth for its weight than any synthetic insulation yet devised, and it compresses into a smaller bundle. In addition, down is wonderfully soft, draping comfortably around your body in ways that the lower-grade synthetics can't begin to match. If you take good care of a down bag, it will retain its loft far longer than a synthetic one. The only synthetic bag I've owned, which was filled with a DuPont insulation called Quallofil, lost about half its loft in three years. However, if you find that you retire bags after three or four years because the shell has become stained or ripped, then spending the money on a long-lasting fill may be a waste.

Down's negatives are equally clear. As I found out in chilling fashion on Mount Huntington, a down bag collapses and loses all its loft when it gets soaked. Data from DuPont show that the insulation value of a Quallofil bag drops 15 percent when it has absorbed 25 percent of its weight in water. The insulation of a down bag drops 50 percent. A down bag also dries more slowly than a synthetic one and costs considerably more initially, although its cost per year, given good care, may actually be lower because of its longer life.

Down quality is measured by the quantity of space that can be filled by one ounce of down. Very-low-quality down may fill 450 cubic inches per ounce, a number so low that many places selling such gear won't even give the down a number. These days, you're better off buying a synthetic bag than one filled with 450-cubic-inch down. Medium-quality down lofts about 550 cubic inches per ounce. The best synthetics now claim to rival 550-fill down. No synthetic, however, can yet claim to equal 650-fill down, the highest quality—and most expensive—down available regularly in sleeping bags.

It's fun to own the best gear, but you should keep in mind what the weight difference between 550- and 650-fill down really amounts to. On a sleeping bag rated to be comfortable down to 20°, (a typical summer-weight backpacking bag), using 650 down instead of 550 saves less than a quarter of a pound, or about as much as a fancy Swiss Army knife or substantial liverwurst sandwich. On a full-blown, keep-you-warm-when-hell's-freezing-over expedition bag rated to –40°, it saves you about half a pound.

Your best assurance that the down you buy really will loft as advertised is the reputation of the manufacturer and the shop. There's no way that you, as a consumer, can independently test the manufacturer's claims. However, you can sometimes distinguish low-grade down from higher-grade down by the feel. A cheap down bag will often contain feathers as well as down. Feathers don't provide the same amount of loft that down does, and they break down much faster. A bag containing a significant amount of feathers will feel stiff, as though it contains straw. Don't be seduced by labels like "prime, northern, gray, or white," which have no legal definition and aren't necessarily an indicator of quality. Goose down is normally considered superior to duck down because the down plumules from the larger bird are larger and therefore loftier, but good duck down is better than bad goose down. The stated fill power is your best indication of quality.

ALTERNATIVES TO DOWN

Down's strongest suit has always been its high warmth-to-weight ratio, which far exceeded the original synthetics. In the early 1990s, however, DuPont, 3M, and Hoechst-Celanese introduced several exciting new kinds of insulation that give down its strongest challenge yet on that score. Like the older synthetics, none of the new ones absorb water and all retain their loft when wet, unlike down. Compressibility is getting better and better, and although none are quite as compressible as 650 fill down, they're getting close to 550.

Polarguard, the iron horse of the synthetics, has been upgraded and renamed Polarguard HV. The old Polarguard was a batting made of long, continuous strands of solid polyester, held together by a sprayed-on resin. Polarguard HV from Hoechst-Celanese is identical, except that now the polyester strands are hollow, which increases the loft for a given weight. The new version should continue to have the virtues of the old, which were durability and low cost. Polarguard's drawbacks are its poor compressibility, stiffness, and relatively low warmth to weight ratio, which still doesn't equal 550 fill down.

Lite Loft, from 3M, is a polyester batting held together with a polyolefin binder fiber. What that tech-talk means to the consumer is a more lofty, more compressible and, naturally, more expensive product than Polarguard HV. Lite Loft's warmth-to-weight ratio runs a close second to 550-fill down. Significantly, at least one manufacturer that used to offer 550-fill down bags has dropped them in favor of Lite Loft bags. At the same time, the company upgraded its down bags to 650 fill.

Micro Loft is DuPont's first new insulation since Quallofil was introduced in 1982. This insulation is made entirely of short polyester fibers, about two inches long. Micro Loft's performance is roughly similar to Lite Loft's.

Prima Loft, the last of the new entries, takes a rather different approach to sleeping-bag insulation. All of the other synthetics have sought to emulate down by providing as much loft as possible for their weight. Nonmoving, "dead" air (the best is bottled in Los Angeles during smog alerts) is an excellent insulator, and most sleeping-bag insulations try to trap as much of it as possible. However, high-loft insulators aren't particularly good at stopping the loss of radiant heat. Prima Loft uses dense, very fine fibers ideally suited to just that task. As a result, Prima Loft sleeping bags are much less lofty than sleeping bags of the same warmth that are filled with other materials.

All four of these insulations were frolicking newborns at the time this book went to press. Like the young of any species, all look much cuter than the staid old-timers such as Hollofil 808, Hollofil II and Quallofil, which are still on the market. It seems likely, however, that at least some will age badly or even meet an untimely demise. Again, a good shop is the best source of the most up-to-date information.

TEMPERATURE RATINGS

For most backpackers, an Everest-rated sleeping bag is like a dental appointment: expensive and uncomfortable. Sleeping in a bag that's too warm can be surprisingly miserable. Opening just one side to ventilate is like trying to warm yourself at a fire. The side of you near the zipper freezes, while the side tucked into the bag sweats profusely. Excessively warm bags are also unnecessarily heavy and bulky. Your best bet is to buy a bag rated for the lowest temperature you'll encounter *regularly*. On extra cold nights, wear more clothing. If you become obsessed with winter backpacking, you'll probably want to invest in a full-on winter bag rated to −20° or −30°. For really hot summer conditions, like southern Utah in July, you may need only a sheet in which to wrap yourself, plus a sweater for the wee hours.

The following chart shows approximately how much loft you need to sleep comfortably at a given temperature.

TEMPERATURE IN °F	TOTAL LOFT IN INCHES
40	3
30	4
20	5
10	6
0	7
−10	8
−20	9
−30	10

This chart is about as reliable as the sun rising on February 29th. People differ greatly in their metabolism. Cora, for example, sleeps comfortably beside me in a bag with nearly double the amount of insulation mine has. She uses a bag rated to 0° for summer backpacking even though the temperature almost never dips below freezing, and she's rarely too warm. At the opposite extreme, I've slept in a tent at 17,000 feet on McKinley in a sleeping bag rated to −15° when the temperature outside the tent was −40°. I got some sleep, but I can't say I was terribly comfortable, and I was wearing every scrap of clothing I'd brought, including four pile hats and hoods. People also vary in their need for insulation at different times. If you go to bed wet, cold, exhausted, poorly fed, and dehydrated, you'll need a lot warmer bag to be comfortable than if you go to bed warm, dry and full to the brim with a final cup of hot chocolate.

Nearly all manufacturers supply a temperature rating with their bags. These ratings are based on the manufacturer's estimate of what the average person will need on an average night when the moon is full and Pisces is rising in the east. There's usually nothing very scientific in how they arrive at their guess; and even if there is, your own experience may differ. However, most people can make an educated guess, based on comparison with companions at home and during car-camping trips, whether they sleep warmer or cooler than average. People who always feel like a Popsicle should buy a bag rated to 5° or 10° colder than the average low temperature they expect. People who find themselves frolicking up the trail in shorts when everyone else is swaddled in goose down can probably get away with a bag rated down to 5° or 10° warmer than the average low.

VAPOR BARRIER AND
RADIANT BARRIER LINERS

Winter backpackers can add a lot of warmth to their sleeping bags by using a vapor-barrier liner: a six-foot-long bag made of a waterproof, nonbreathable coated material. A VB liner stops the heat loss caused by evaporation of insensible perspiration, the water you constantly lose through your skin just because your skin is not water-tight like a plastic bag. A VB liner also stops the evaporation of sensible perspiration, the kind you produce when you're overheating, so you need to regulate your temperature carefully by shedding clothing if you start to sweat. Used properly, a VB liner can allow you to sleep comfortably in temperatures 10° or 15° lower than you could without a liner. Used improperly, a VB liner will awaken you with the feeling you've encamped in tropical Borneo.

VB liners provide a crucial additional benefit: they help keep your sleeping bag dry. In severe cold, without a VB liner, the moisture that escapes from your body will condense inside your insulation, whether it's down or a synthetic, reducing its effectiveness. During my second expedition to Alaska, in 1980, the down bags used by my two companions collapsed completely as moisture built up during our thirteen-day epic ascent of the south face of Mount Hunter. Peter Metcalf said later that his bag became so useless he would simply have thrown it away if it hadn't cost so much. During Will Steger's dogsled expedition to the North Pole, the team's synthetic sleeping bags accumulated 35 pounds of ice through condensation because the team wasn't using VB liners. In 1982, when both Peter and I used VB liners inside our bags during our ascent of Reality Ridge on McKinley, both of our bags stayed dry and lofty, in large part because of the liners, but also because we took every possible opportunity to dry our bags.

While preparing for an Alaskan expedition in 1983, I took the vapor-barrier concept into the realm of fanaticism and decided I needed to back up the coated nylon VB liner I normally used with a giant plastic bag. Unfortunately, the requisite size of bag was only available in 100-bag rolls. Fortunately, I was able to persuade a friend to share the purchase of a roll. Even more fortunately, my friend remained my friend after this rather shameless imposition in an obsessive cause. A normal coated nylon vapor barrier is all you really need, even in severe cold. Summer backpackers need not concern themselves with vapor barriers at all.

For a time in the early 1980s, manufacturers experimented with a different kind of liner, one designed to block the loss of heat in the form of infrared radiation. Texolite was the most common brand name. The material did indeed prove its worth in the synthetic sleeping bags of the day, where adding the weight of the liner provided more additional warmth than adding an equivalent weight of insulation. The same was not true of good down bags, however, where a user needing additional warmth was better off adding more down than adding Texolite.

Texolite's problem, at least in the minds of summer users, was that the material was also a pretty effective vapor barrier. People complained that Texolite bags had too limited a comfort range: They found themselves overheating too easily. Partisans of vapor barriers like equipment designer Jack Stephenson would argue that all these complainers wanted was the license to sweat and soak their insulation, and that the better solution would have been for overheated users to take off some clothing. Despite such cogent arguments, however, the consumer rules in our society, and Texolite and its competitors have gone the way of the dodo, at least for now.

SIZE, SHAPE, AND FIT

Your sleeping bag's shape and fit greatly influence its warmth. Form-fitting bags contoured to fit a human body are called mummies because, like your mother when you were a kid, they hug you close and keep you warm. (Actually, they were named for the preserved bodies of dead Egyptians, which they resemble in shape, but I'd rather fall asleep thinking about *my* definition than the real one.) More expansive bags, for those of substantial girth or those who like more wiggle room, are known variously as wide mummies or barrels (I can see my mother frowning); even more capacious bags are known as semirectangular bags. Fully rectangular bags (named, of course, for really square moms) are for slumber parties and warm-weather car camping. They're too bulky and heavy for backpacking.

Snug-fitting bags are generally warmer than loose-fitting ones, in part because there is less cold air and icy sleeping bag surrounding you when you first climb in, so the bags warm up faster. More importantly, a snug-fitting bag, combined with an effective hood, helps prevent your movements from pumping warm air out of the mouth of the bag, then drawing in cold air. Too snug, however, will give you claustrophobia, so be sure to slip inside the bag at the shop before buying. Most good shops will let you try on a bag if you take off your shoes and look civilized. Many winter campers like to buy an extralong bag to provide room at the foot for items that should be kept from freezing, such as water bottles, boots, and cameras.

Several more details are worth considering. A hood is an integral part of all good mummy bags. It's designed so that tightening a drawstring cinches down the bag's mouth until only your face is exposed. In addition to a hood, good winter bags often have an

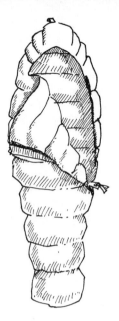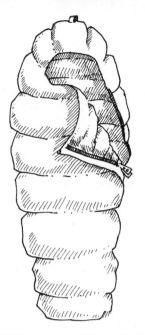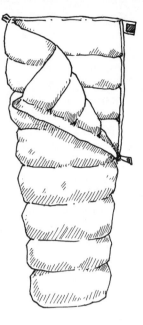

THE THREE STYLES OF SLEEPING BAGS—
MUMMY, WIDE MUMMY, AND
RECTANGULAR—ARE FOR BACKPACKERS
RANGING FROM WEIGHT CONSCIOUS TO
CLAUSTROPHOBIC.

insulation-filled collar that closes down over your shoulders and around your neck to further reduce the escape of warm air. Most bags are supplied with full-length zippers to make it easier to get in and out of them. That zipper can be another avenue of heat loss unless it's protected by a draft tube; a long, insulation-filled tube on the inside of the bag that covers the zipper. Cold feet seem to be a perennial problem on chilly nights. Better bags often have extra insulation in the foot area. Don't worry unduly about the other details of construction, such as which particular baffle system is used in a down bag, or whether a synthetic bag is described as having shingle or double-overlapping quilt construction. All of the methods used by reputable manufacturers work just fine.

Most sleeping bags have an outer shell of porous nylon that makes no claim to be waterproof. Even as a novice, I knew that sleeping unprotected in the rain would guarantee a soaking wet bag. But what about in winter? Shouldn't it be possible to sleep in the open, since it would be so cold that snow wouldn't melt on the bag? Such a tactic, if successful, would save the weight of a tent during winter climbs.

In 1977, Joe Kaelin and I set out to test that theory on our first effort to climb a major route in Rocky Mountain National Park in winter. Already impressed with the cold, we bivouacked at the base of the face under a boulder, then started up the climb at first light. Darkness caught us only halfway up the route, and we searched futilely for some kind of sheltered bivouac site. At last we gave up, scooped out two body-sized ledges in the midst of an unprotected gully, and crawled into our bags.

At midnight I awoke feeling that my sleeping bag had grown tremendously heavy. Spindrift pouring down the narrow slot above us had completely buried our bags. I pushed away the snow as best I could from inside the bag and tried to go back to sleep, but in vain. Two hours later, with sleep impossible and our bags rapidly becoming drenched, we began soloing up the face by headlamp. We summited a few hours after sunrise.

As we had demonstrated so convincingly, enough heat escapes through your sleeping bag to melt snow or frost lying on the shell fabric. You don't need to do anything as foolish as exposing your bag to a nonstop spindrift cascade to get your bag damp in the winter. Frost sifts down from tent walls, while spindrift blows in each time the door is opened. Meltwater drips from snow-cave roofs while wind carries snow into the entrance. Even in summer, condensation dripping from tent walls can dampen your bag gradually. A sleeping bag with a waterproof-breathable Gore-Tex shell will help keep your bag dry. Gore-Tex-shelled bags are also a bit warmer because of the windproofness of the Gore-Tex, but I wouldn't buy a Gore-Tex bag just for that reason.

If you and your mate are like otters, who like to sleep half on top of each other, you may be interested in buying sleeping bags that can zip together into one giant love-nest. One bag must have a right-hand zipper, the other a left. In addition, the zippers must be the same size. Most sleeping-bag manufacturers offer bags that will zip together. Highly compatible couples could also buy a semirectangular bag that can be unzipped completely so that it lies flat like a comforter. The unfolded bag is then zipped to a simple cotton or nylon sheet with a zipper along its perimeter. The result is, again, a giant love-nest, but this time one that has insulation only on top. The sheets that make this transformation possible are known variously as doublers, couplers, or couplets. The advantage of a doubler is that it lets you carry sleeping gear for two that weighs just a pound more than sleeping gear for one. Cora and I find that doublers work well down to about 40° or so. Below that, we sleep cold because it's impossible to cinch down the mouth of the bag to prevent the escape of warm air.

SLEEPING PADS

Regardless of the sleeping bag you choose, the insulation will always smash flat beneath you. To prevent a close encounter with the cold, stony ground, you need a sleeping pad.

As a kid, you may have slept in your backyard on a slab of open-cell foam or a 3-inch-thick air-mattress that made you dizzy as a top from the effort of inflating it. If either of these two items is still lingering in your closet, let it linger. Open-cell foam—the kind that crushes under body weight to about one-quarter of its original thickness—is generally too heavy, water absorbing, and bulky for backpacking. Normal air mattresses, while comfortable in warm weather, are chilly when the ground is cold because air circulates freely inside them, drawing heat from your body through convection.

For years, all I ever used as a sleeping pad while backpacking in the summer was a sheet of half-inch-thick closed-cell foam. Closed-cell foam is lightweight and cheap, doesn't absorb water, and is highly durable. It's also rather uncomfortable to sleep on if you, like me, have spent years being spoiled on an acre-wide modern home mattress. In the backcountry I always secretly envied my friends the luxury afforded by their Therm-A-Rests—essentially, air mattresses filled with open-cell foam—even as I derided them as heavy, leak prone, even a touch bourgeois. My friends just smiled, indulging me in my tirades. Finally, my inflated ego collapsed under the complaints of my bruised hips, and Cora and I bought a pair of Therm-A-Rests.

What luxury! Sure, they weigh 2 pounds 5 ounces each rather than 10 ounces like my old closed-cell foam pad, but the comfort is worth it (or maybe I'm just so much more tired after lugging the extra weight up the trail that I could sleep on porcupine hide). The open-cell foam prevents convection, so the pads are warm, while the waterproof, airtight shell keeps the foam dry. After our first tantalizing taste of backwoods luxury, Cora and I plunged further into decadence and bought Therm-A-Rest Chairs, 10-ounce fabric and webbing devices that convert a Therm-A-Rest into a legless chair that sits directly on the ground. No more aching backs while cooking dinner or lazing about watching the sunset! Therm-A-Rest is no longer the only brand of foam-filled air mattress available, but it does have a proven track record. A leaky or inferior brand could prove to be a letdown.

I find a pillow even more essential for comfortable sleep in the woods than I do at home. Rather than carry an actual pillow, I stuff an extra sweater into my sleeping-bag stuff sack, the stout nylon bag that comes with every decent sleeping bag.

SLEEPING-BAG CARE

Caring for your sleeping bag starts with proper storage. Never store your bag by stuffing it into its stuff sack and tossing it in the closet: the sustained compression of the insulation, whether down or a synthetic, will cause the bag to lose its loft. Instead, store your bag by hanging it in a closet or by placing it in the extra-large storage sack sold by most sleeping-bag manufacturers. Heat and compression combined are worse than compression alone. Don't store your stuffed bag in the trunk of your car during the summer.

You can also prolong your bag's life by keeping it clean. That means always sleeping in a tent or on a groundsheet, not directly on dirt, and wearing clothing when you go to bed. It's a lot easier to wash long underwear than it is to wash a sleeping bag. Spot-clean stained areas as soon as possible after they get dirty, rather than washing the entire bag. Airing your bag in the sun for a few hours after each trip will help kill any musty odors that develop.

When your entire bag finally does need washing, usually after several seasons of hard use, take it to a commercial laundromat with a large-capacity, *front-loading* washing machine. Do not use a top-loading, agitator-type machine, which can easily ruin your bag through rough handling. Front-loading machines tumble your bag and put much less stress on batts of synthetic insulation and the fragile baffles that hold your down in place. Use a soap that dissolves well in the local water. Your goal is not only to get soap into the bag to get it clean, but to get *all* the soap back out. Soap residues in any bag can cause clumping of the insulation and loss of loft. Special down soaps dissolve easily and rinse out well, but aren't really necessary and may not be strong enough to remove stains from the shell. Drycleaning is not advisable. Some experts argue that drycleaning strips oil from down and makes it brittle. Others argue that few drycleaners take the care to make sure that all the dissolved dirt is rinsed out of the bag with clean solvent. In any case, the fumes from solvent residues can give you headaches, or worse.

If you must wash your bag at home, fill a bathtub with warm water and a little soap. Immerse the bag gently, knead the soapy water into the bag, then drain and rinse repeatedly until no more soap bubbles percolate through the shell. Press—don't wring—the water from the bag and lift it gently from the tub. Wet down is heavy, and the weight of it can rip the baffles loose from their moorings if the bag is manhandled. Dry the bag in a tumble dryer on low heat, which can take several hours. Be sure the bag is thoroughly dry before storing it. You may need to fluff a down bag vigorously to break up clumps of down and restore the full loft. Think of this as an exercise in feathering your own nest.

BACKCOUNTRY STOVES

"Fire is the best of servants; but what a
master!"

—Thomas Carlyle, *Past and Present,* 1843

A s someone who reviews equipment regularly for a major outdoors magazine, I've had the privilege of experimenting with a
wide variety of recently introduced equipment, including, on
several particularly thrilling occasions, new stoves. The incident that provoked the most excitement occurred when I was review-
ing a new multi-fuel stove from a company that shall remain nameless,
since they fixed the problem with remarkable haste. Ostensibly, this
stove was capable of burning both white gas and kerosene. I filled the
stove with white gas while it was sitting in the middle of my concrete
driveway, well away from important flammable structures like my
garage, and fired it up. No problem. I shut it down, drained the remaining white gas back into its one-gallon steel storage container and,
like a flaming idiot, left the lid off the container. For equally inexplica-
ble reasons, I now moved the scene of operations to my front porch—I
was still operating on concrete, mind you, but now was only about
three feet from another important flammable. structure, namely, my
front door. I filled the innocent-looking stove with kerosene, pumped it
up as directed, opened the valve, and flicked my Bic. A wispy flame
sprang to life. I pumped again, and suddenly liquid kerosene flooded

the burner. A miniature fireball erupted, with flames shooting three feet high. I grabbed the stove by its base, knowing it would only remain cool to the touch for another few seconds, and heaved the stove into the middle of my concrete driveway. Sandy Koufax couldn't have made the pitch to home more accurately—the flaming stove landed within inches of the wide-open, nearly full can of explosively volatile white gas. I sprinted down the steps of my front porch, snatched away the can of white gas, and stood there shaking as the broken and battered stove gradually sputtered out.

I called the company and immediately launched into an apology for breaking this marvelous example of American craftsmanship that they had entrusted me with, but only managed to utter a sentence before I was interrupted by the *spokeswoman's* profuse apology. They had just discovered, somewhat belatedly, that the stove's design was defective.

The moral, of course, is that the only difference between men and boys is the flammability of their toys. Seriously, all backpacking stoves can be dangerous if used by careless or ignorant people. Learn your stove's idiosyncrasies thoroughly by practicing with it in a safe place where nothing nearby can be damaged if the stove leaks and catches fire.

Once upon a time, when backpacking stoves (and backpackers) were scarce and firewood was plentiful, everyone cooked over an open flame. As I'll explain further in Chapter 11, those days are gone forever in nearly all parts of the country. In many prime backpacking locations, campfires are illegal, immoral, and maybe even fattening. Good backpacking stoves today are inexpensive, readily available, and essential to preserving the wilderness feel of what little wild land still exists.

WHITE-GAS STOVES

Before selecting a particular model of stove, you must first decide what type of fuel you want to burn. North American backpackers have two main choices: white gas and butane. Both fuels have strong advantages and distinct drawbacks.

The main advantage of white-gas stoves is high heat output in all conditions, even in severe cold. A minor advantage is the lower cost of the fuel compared to butane cartridges, but few people spend enough time backpacking for the cost to make much difference. (As an aside, white gas, more accurately known as naphtha, is *not* the same as automotive gasoline, either leaded or unleaded. Trying to burn automotive gas in a white-gas-only stove will result in rapid clogging of the burner orifice where the vaporized fuel emerges and ignites.) The disadvantages of white-gas stoves are the inconvenience of lighting them, the racket they produce when they're burning, and the greater

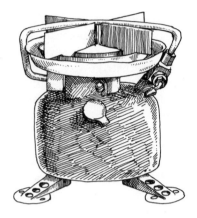

ONE MODEL OF A
WHITE-GAS STOVE.

amount of maintenance they require. White gas is extremely volatile, which means that spills evaporate readily, without leaving an oily residue like kerosene does. It also means that accidentally igniting a spilled pool of fuel would cause a disastrous fireball that would make my little epic seem like a candle-lighting ceremony.

A modern white-gas stove consists of a tank to hold the fuel, a pump to create pressure in the tank so the fuel will flow out through the fuel line, a valve to control fuel flow, and a burner assembly where the gas mixes with air and burns.

To burn efficiently, white gas must be vaporized by heat. Once the stove is running, vaporization takes place in the fuel line as the line passes directly through the flames emitted by the burner. The vaporized fuel then burns, vaporizing more fuel, and the cycle is completed. The trick is getting the cycle going. To do that, most white-gas stoves must be primed, which is tech-talk for preheating the fuel line by releasing a teaspoon of fuel into a small depression at the base of the burner, then igniting it. The easiest way to get the priming fuel in place is to give the pump a dozen strokes, then open the valve a crack, which lets a small amount of liquid fuel escape through the orifice and dribble down to the priming cup. Priming with white gas is a potentially dangerous maneuver that must be executed with great care well away from anything flammable. If you use too much priming fuel, the stove will flare up. Coleman's Peak 1 white-gas stove is one model that doesn't need to be primed unless the temperature is below freezing. An alternative to priming with white gas is carrying a small squeeze bottle of stove alcohol or a tube of priming paste. Neither alcohol nor priming paste will flare up as an excessive amount of white gas will.

You may occasionally run across old white-gas stoves that lack a pump. Do not be tempted to buy them. These ancient geezers are

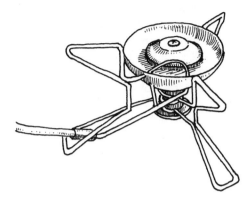

ANOTHER MODEL OF A WHITE-GAS STOVE.

supposedly "self-pressurizing," meaning that the heat of the flame was supposed to keep the tank hot enough to maintain sufficient pressure inside for the stove to continue operating. Set the stove on cold ground, however, and you could gradually lose pressure and heat output. The pump found on all modern white-gas stoves makes the whole operation a lot less finicky because you can reliably add pressure to the tank whenever you need it. For years, the best white-gas and multi-fuel backpacking stoves on the market have been made by MSR and Coleman's Peak 1 division. If you choose to buy a white-gas stove, select a model from either of these two companies, and you won't go far wrong.

The orifices on white-gas stoves need periodic cleaning, particularly if you're burning kerosene. The second most common failure

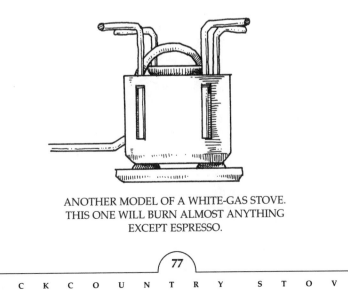

ANOTHER MODEL OF A WHITE-GAS STOVE.
THIS ONE WILL BURN ALMOST ANYTHING
EXCEPT ESPRESSO.

point for white-gas stoves is the pump cup, which needs oiling periodically with two or three drops of a lightweight oil. In addition, white-
gas stoves have a variety of rubber seals and gaskets, which need
replacing on occasion. MSR and Coleman both sell spare parts for their
stoves, which should be considered as essential as the stove itself. One
final tip: don't store fuel in the stove's tank. It can become gummy if the
stove sits around unused for several months. Instead, light the stove
and burn off the remaining fuel before storing the stove at the end of
the season. Don't pour unused fuel down the drain or into the gutter,
where it will become a highly toxic pollutant.

BUTANE STOVES

The major advantage of butane stoves is simplicity. Essentially,
they contain three parts: a canister of compressed butane gas, a valve,
and a burner. To light a butane stove, you flick your lighter and open
the valve. The stoves are mercifully quiet, and there's no priming to
worry about, no liquid fuel to spill and essentially no maintenance to
do. I've used butane stoves almost exclusively since 1982, and never
seen one break down. Butane stoves are not idiot-proof, but the average terminally confused backpacker has a hard time making them
malfunction. By contrast, almost every backpacker can tell you a story
about a white-gas stove that became cantankerous.

Butane stoves require no routine maintenance. On expeditions,
I've always carried an orifice-cleaning tool (a stiff, tiny wire attached to
a handle) to clean the orifice where the butane gas emerges, but I've
never needed to use it.

A TYPICAL BUTANE
STOVE.

The main disadvantage of butane stoves is poor heat output in cold weather. Butane stoves work only if the cartridge is warm enough for the butane inside to vaporize into energetic little gas molecules that are eager to flow out the nozzle and burn. Normal butane condenses to a liquid at 31°. Stoves burning normal butane produce practically no heat below that temperature because very little butane gas flows out through the burner when the valve is opened. Fortunately, cartridges are now available for the Camping Gaz Bleuet 206, the most common model of butane stove, which contain a mixture of propane and butane. Propane liquefies at −44°, so the combined fuel works much better than normal butane in severe cold. MSR and other manufacturers offer stoves that burn isobutane, a variety of butane that liquefies at 11°. These stoves also work better in the cold than normal butane stoves. High altitude, with its lower air pressure, further increases the output of butane stoves compared to their performance at sea level. Just as water boils (vaporizes) at a lower temperature as you go higher, so too do butane and its variants. A lower boiling point means more butane gas flows out at a given temperature. You'll get much better performance at 14,300 feet on McKinley at 0°, for example, than you will during a January cold snap in Arches National Park at 5,200 feet.

I now do nearly all of my backpacking in the spring, summer and fall in the United States. For me, the simplicity and ease of use of a butane stove, particularly now that the butane/propane cartridges are available, makes it the stove of choice. However, I grant you that using a butane stove successfully in the wintertime at normal altitudes, even with the new fuels, requires rather heroic measures involving hanging-stove setups, homemade insulation for the cartridge and copper tubing to conduct heat from the flame down to the cartridge. In really desperate situations, I've found myself warming the cartridge with a cigarette lighter, a potentially dangerous practice akin to squirting charcoal lighter onto already-burning charcoal. If you plan to do a lot of cold-weather backpacking in the United States, buy a white-gas stove.

Adventurous backpackers planning to trek through Nepal, Patagonia or Outer Mongolia will find that white gas is generally unavailable outside the United States, while stores carrying butane-filled Camping Gaz Bleuet cartridges are surprisingly widespread (well, maybe not in Outer Mongolia). Kerosene is available universally, but the quality varies widely and it must be filtered carefully. Several stoves on the market today can be easily modified to burn either kerosene or white gas. The modification usually requires a screwdriver or wrench and an inexpensive, manufacturer-supplied part. Airline regulations prohibit carrying fuel of any type on board, so you'll have to plan on obtaining it once you arrive.

POTS AND PANS

Selecting the rest of your kitchen kit is easy if you backpack in the style that Cora and I do. We like to spend our time hiking, searching for subjects to photograph and watching the marmots pout and the pikas scold, rather than slaving over a stove in camp trying to prepare a gourmet meal. We bring just one five-cup pot. In addition, we each carry a metal spoon, a plastic mug with a lid, and a plastic bowl which, in its former incarnation was a margarine container. A pair of sturdy pot grips, available in backpacking shops, is another essential. To be sure, some backpackers choose to make the preparation and consumption of delicacies the central point of their trip. They bring a Teflon frying pan for the trout they hope to catch and a griddle to bake their pancakes. They buy a lightweight collapsible oven that uses a backpacking stove as the heat source, and turn out miniature pizzas and brownies alongside the shores of high-country lakes. We choose to burden ourselves with extra lenses instead of pots and pans, but that's the beauty of backpacking: there's room out there for fanatics of every persuasion. And room, too, for those sane souls who can shrug off their city obsessions and just enjoy the wilderness for what it is.

8

MISCELLANEOUS ESSENTIALS

"My candle burns at both ends;
It will not last the night;
But, ah, my foes, and oh, my friends,
It gives a lovely light."

—Edna St. Vincent Millay, "First Fig," 1920

Three friends—Lisa Cotter, Jenny Ball, and Cindy Carey—were planning an expedition to Mount McKinley, a peak which is infamous for the arctic gales that beset its slopes. Accordingly, they wanted to get some experience camping in high winds. They decided, a bit naïvely, that the ideal location for a training trip was the Boulderfield on Longs Peak in Rocky Mountain National Park. The Boulderfield is a bleak, rocky plain, far above timberline, that is raked by hurricane-force winds in the wintertime. One stormy February weekend, a few months before the expedition, they invited me to join them and we headed up. Winter days go fast, and the last pink glow of sunset was abandoning the peaks to the north when we finally got the tents erect in the stiff wind and crawled inside. Jenny and I, together in one tent, cooked dinner by the light of our headlamps. I noticed that the battery powering my headlamp was growing weak. No worries, I thought; we're only here one night, I'll only need my headlamp for another few minutes and besides, I have a spare battery. Soon after the last sip of hot chocolate, we doused the headlamps and plunged the tent into darkness. The wind began to grow stronger. The tent strained against the gusts as the taut fabric crackled noisely. I had been dozing restlessly for no more than half an hour when a loud snap! like a breaking tree limb jarred me awake. The wind had broken one of the tent poles. An instant later the second one, now unsupported, fractured as well and the tent began flapping and billowing like a giant jellyfish gone mad. I lunged for my headlamp and flicked it on to survey the damage. The beam faintly illuminated a gaping rip in the fabric. Afraid the tent would be destroyed completely and all of our extra gear would blow away, Jenny and I began packing frantically. Suddenly my headlamp winked out, its battery shot. Fumbling in the dark, I plugged in my spare battery, confident that our lack of light was merely a temporary annoyance. Then I discovered that it, too, had somehow become drained. A minute later, Jenny's headlamp failed as well. Fortunately, she also had a spare battery. Unfortunately, it, too, was dead. Embarrassed now as well as desperate, we borrowed a headlamp from Cindy and Lisa, finished stowing our gear, and packed up the tattered remnants of the tent. Cindy and Lisa's tent had also suffered a broken pole; a second pole was bent badly, but the tent, although lopsided, was still standing. The four of us squeezed inside and waited for dawn. When morning finally arrived, we abandoned our plans to climb Longs Peak and scurried for home.

HEADLAMPS

Our experience illustrates the first law of nighttime disaster control: no headlamp is reliable unless you check the batteries—and the spares—in advance. Electronics stores usually sell inexpensive battery testers that work with all sizes of batteries. I bought mine (belatedly) at Radio Shack. Battery testers can tell you only whether the battery is good or not; they can't tell you how much life is left, since some batteries, like nicads, put out nearly their full voltage until exhausted. Alkalines lose power in a more linear fashion, so a battery tester can give you some idea of an alkaline's remaining life, but it's still an educated guess, at best. When in doubt, pack two sets of spares. Spare bulbs are equally important. If we hadn't been able to borrow a headlamp from Lisa and Cindy, Jenny and I would have been in much worse trouble. The odds would have been good that some valuable piece of equipment would have blown away in the dark as we struggled to pack all our gear. It just goes to show that when darkness reigns, a headlamp is delight.

If you're a typical summer backpacker, you'll never need to worry about your tent exploding around your ears, but you're quite likely to need a reliable headlamp or flashlight, if only to investigate those mysterious midnight gnawing sounds that prove to be a por-

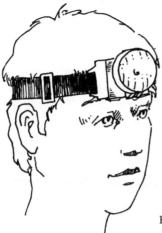

USING A HEADLAMP KEEPS YOUR
HANDS FREE FOR COOKING OR FOR
PITCHING A TENT.

cupine chewing into your pack.

A headlamp is just a bulb and a reflector mounted on an elastic headband. With some models, the battery case is also attached to the headband; with others, it rides in a pocket, where the battery stays warmer and therefore lasts longer. The disadvantage of that system, of course, is that you then have a wire running from a pocket to your head, which not only makes you look like an android, but also gives malicious branches the perfect handle to rip your headlamp from your head. Headlamps let you use both hands to pitch your tent, cook, or pack, which is why Cora and I prefer them over flashlights. For trail walking, however, you'll often find that carrying the headlamp in your hands makes it easier to pick out obstacles in the trail. The reason? Moving the light away from your eyes gives better definition to the scene by casting longer and more pronounced shadows.

The best batteries for the environment and for your pocketbook over the long run are rechargeable nicads. They cost more initially, and you have to buy a battery charger as well, but they have a useful life of 500 to 1,000 charges, which makes them far more economical over time. One disadvantage is that nicads hold less energy than comparable alkaline batteries. A second disadvantage is that even fully charged, never-used nicads will gradually go dead over a period of two or three months and have to be recharged. Disposable alkaline batteries are convenient because of their long shelf life, but they contain nasty acids and heavy metals that pollute groundwater if these toxins seep out through the bottom of a landfill. In cold weather, nicads have the advantage over alkalines because their power output doesn't drop off as fast as alkalines' power does. The best batteries for really severe cold, however, are the nonrechargeable lithiums. Nothing else will power a headlamp reliably at temperatures below 0.

OTHER ESSENTIALS

A checklist of backpacking gear inevitably contains a host of other small but essential items. For example, Cora and I each carry a Swiss Army knife. The model we like has two knife blades, a can opener, scissors, tweezers, and a corkscrew. Carrying a knife lets you spread your peanut butter on a bagel, open a can of tuna, trim frayed fabric that keeps jamming in a zipper, pull a splinter, and pop the cork on a bottle of wine, should your party include a strong-backed soul willing to carry it.

To light your stove, you'll need either a cigarette lighter or matches. Cora and I carry both because lighters, although convenient, have a disconcerting habit of failing if the lighter gets wet or the operator's hands are damp. Matches provide an excellent backup if they're carefully secured inside a plastic bag without holes. For even greater security, you can find waterproof, strike-anywhere matches in backpacking stores. It's a good idea to throw an extra cigarette lighter into the repair kit or some other secure place, just in case.

People whose boots are heavy or uncomfortable sometimes bring a pair of lightweight slippers or sandals to change into once they reach camp. People whose feet are chronically cold in their sleeping bags at night may enjoy a pair of down booties. On snowy trips, it's convenient to have some means of walking around in the snow without having to put your stiff, heavy ski boots or mountaineering boots back on. One solution on really cold trips is bringing insulated nylon overboots. During the day, you wear the overboots over your regular boots. Overboots cover up the lugged boot sole, so you'll also need to use skis, crampons, or snowshoes to provide traction as you travel. At night, you can slip on the overboots alone when you just need to step outside the tent to perform some chore. Another solution at night is to put a heavy-duty stuff sack over either your inner boots (if you normally wear double boots) or over your socks. If you use a big stuff sack, such as the one containing your sleeping bag, the stuff sack will reach to your knees. You can keep the stuff sack from falling down around your ankles by tightening the cord lock on the stuff sack's drawstring. On Alaskan expeditions, I sometimes brought two extra stuff sacks for just this purpose. Just be sure you stay off any hard-packed snow slopes while wearing your stuff sacks. I still remember stepping out of my tent at 17,200 feet on McKinley's West Buttress and immediately slipping, falling, and sliding 20 feet down the wind-packed snow. I stood up, unhurt, took one step back toward the tent and immediately fell down again. Returning to the tent was impossible until I hit on the idea of just removing the stuff sacks. My textured wool socks gripped the polished snow securely, and I walked back to the tent with ease.

Summer backpackers in wooded regions rarely need sunglasses. However, if you're hiking above timberline across early summer's lingering snowfields, sunglasses can prevent a lot of uncomfortable squinting or worse. Snowblindness—essentially, sunburn of the cornea of the eye—can cause severe pain for several days. Don't count on pain to warn you of the danger, however; the pain begins several hours after the damage is done. If you find yourself squinting heavily, you should put on your sunglasses. Time is the only cure for snowblindness, although victims normally get some relief by remaining in a darkened room or otherwise shielding their eyes from light. Desert hikers frequently find sunglasses a pleasure, and winter backpackers in snow country should routinely carry both sunglasses and goggles. In an emergency, almost any way of reducing the amount of light hitting your eyes will help. I once cut a slit in my wilderness permit to make an impromptu pair of sunglasses. On another occasion, after my first and only bout of snowblindness, I taped up my goggles so that only a slit remained. The system relieved some of the pain, but made skiing interesting, since I could only see one narrow strip of snow at a time. People who have eyesight so poor that they would have trouble hiking out if their glasses were broken should bring a spare pair.

A large plastic garbage bag slipped over your pack with the mouth pointing down will keep your pack dry during a nighttime shower. You can use a bit of duct tape from your repair kit to patch minor rips and extend the bag's useful life.

After Cora had $4,000 worth of dental work done a couple of years ago, we became remarkably conscientious about bringing toothbrushes, toothpaste, and floss on all our backpacking trips, even short ones. Our personal hygiene kit also contains (at Cora's insistence) a package of premoistened towelettes and a hairbrush. Even I insist on bringing toilet paper, unlike some hard-cores I know. A trowel is valuable for burying wastes (more on this subject later).

Embarrassed as I may be to admit my addiction to a quintessentially citified piece of gear, I find a watch to be an important item of wilderness equipment. I use it primarily to keep track of our pace and timing. Will we make the campsite by dark? Will we make the top of the pass in time to shoot the sunrise? A watch also lets you time the cooking of your pasta and rice.

A simple repair kit can save you a lot of grief even on a short trip. A basic kit might include:

- spare parts for the stove
- a little duct tape or ripstop repair tape to patch a hole in a tent, rain jacket, insulated parka or sleeping bag
- extra clevis pins (short aluminum pins that pass through the pack frame

BUYING AN ICE AX

A s I emphasized in the mountaineering-boot sidebar in Chapter 3, mountaineering is a sport that demands respect, proper training, and the right equipment. Among the items you'll need if you venture onto steep snowfields is an ice ax, a tool which actually bears little resemblance to its wood-chopping cousin. As you can see in the illustration, an ice ax has four parts: the shaft, normally made of extruded aluminum tubing; the pick, which the climber drives into the ice or hard snow with the force of his swing; the adze, used to chop out ledges to stand on while resting or belaying; and the spike, which helps the shaft penetrate hard snow and prevents the ax from slipping when it's used as a walking stick. If you will primarily be climbing snow, you want an ice ax that's long enough to reach comfortably from your hand to the ground so you can lean on it effectively. An ice ax designed for climbing frozen waterfalls, on the other hand, will have a shorter shaft and a differently shaped pick that is designed to hook into rotten or multi-layered ice. Ice-climbing tools are a poor bet for snowclimbing because the shaft isn't long enough to serve effectively as a cane.

On a gentle snowfield, a snow-climber's ice ax is used mostly as a walking stick. As the slope steepens, climbers plunge the shaft in as far as it will go and grasp the head of the ice ax to steady themselves while they kick steps. As the snow

and a grommet on the pack bag) and split rings (if you're carrying an external frame pack which uses those devices to attach the pack bag to the frame)

⚑ bit of extra string to use as spare shoelaces and for lashing this to that

A more elaborate repair kit for a trip lasting a week or longer might also contain:

⚑ wire for lashing together broken whatevers

⚑ needle-nose pliers with wirecutters to force the aforementioned wire into place

⚑ heavy-duty sewing awl (Speedy Stitcher is my favorite brand), stout thread and scrap of heavy fabric

hardens and turns to ice, climbers grasp the shaft of the ax near the spike and drive the pick into the snow with a stout swing. If the climber slips, he grabs the head of the ax with one hand and the shaft with the other, then presses the pick into the snow to brake himself to a stop, a technique called self-arrest.

Mastering the use of an ice ax cannot be learned through reading. Seek competent instruction from experienced guides or very competent friends before attempting to climb steep snow.

AN ICE AX IS AN ESSENTIAL TOOL FOR SNOW- AND ICE-CLIMBERS.

⚠ 5-inch length of copper pipe with an inside diameter just larger than the diameter of your tent poles, to patch a broken pole

If you've been clutching your wallet ever more tightly as you read chapter after chapter on what to buy, it's time to relax. With the exception of first-aid kits and water-purification devices, we're done discussing what you need to own. Now, with the buying spree behind us, we can move on to everyone's favorite topic: what's for dinner.

A PROVISIONAL GUIDE TO BACKCOUNTRY FOOD

"An army marches on its stomach."

—Napoleon Bonaparte (attributed), 1769–1821

My early wilderness adventures were noted for their culinary disasters. I did my first backpacking trips with my father in the days when backpacking food was simply dried. Not freeze-dried, mind you; just dried, dehydrated, in reality, fossilized. Resurrecting the dried food of that era into something palatable was about as likely as raising *Tyrannosaurus rex* from the dead. I still remember boiling little chunks of dried carrot for hours and finally consuming them with a frustrating crunch. Then there was the time we set out to make an omelet and mixed up half a packet of dried eggs— but mistakenly used a full measure of water, thus creating a nightmare version of egg-drop soup. Even more memorable, because it was actually planned and therefore inexcusable, was the horse fodder Joe Kaelin and I brought along for breakfast on an insanely windy Thanksgiving trip into Rocky Mountain National Park. (It's the only time I've ever been blown over flat while *kneeling.*) Joe, an impoverished college student with some misguided aspirations to healthy eating habits, thought he would relish oatmeal—raw oatmeal, soaked briefly in watery powdered milk instead of actually cooking it. To no one's surprise but our own, we ended up carrying half of our oatmeal back out again. That we ate any at all is a tribute to the victory of tyrannical stomachs over rebellious taste buds.

With such lessons under our belt, so to speak, my comrades-in-arms and I gradually learned what we could carry, what we could actually cook, and most importantly, what we would actually eat while far away from refrigerators, microwave ovens and telephone hot lines to our favorite pizzeria.

One of the first things we learned is that beginners' eyes are much bigger than their stomachs. There is, quite naturally, a real fear of running out of food when the nearest supermarket is not minutes away, but rather many hours, possibly even days. The almost irresistible temptation is to bring far more food than anyone could consume. Hiking out at the end of a trip with half your food supply still burdening your pack will quickly teach you how much food you actually need for a few days in the wilds.

The errors encouraged by the eyeball method of packing provisions are compounded by the difference between city foods and backpacking foods. In the city, much of our food already has water in it: fruit, vegetables, meat, soups, stews, milk, all canned foods, etc. In the backcountry, on the other hand, almost everything is brought in dry, and water from a lake or stream is added during preparation or cooking. Dry food, besides being lighter, is usually far more compact than hydrated food. A bag scarcely larger than a football can easily contain enough dry food for three days; yet it looks as if it contains only enough for a three-course dinner.

WEEKEND TRIPS

Worrying about weight and bulk is largely unnecessary if your trip will last only two days. Since you'll probably eat breakfast before you start and dinner after you get out of the mountains, you need to plan only four meals. Over that space of time, almost anything goes: ham and cheese sandwiches for lunch, hamburgers with all the trimmings for dinner, donuts and fresh fruit for breakfast. If you pull the frozen hamburger out of your freezer just before heading for the trail head, it will be nicely thawed (but not spoiled) by dinnertime. In fact, on a weekend trip, there's really no need to cook at all if you don't feel like it. Dinner can be just a continuation of lunch, perhaps with a different filling between the slices of bread. With a little experience, the eyeball method of assessing quantities will work just fine for a two-day trip. Sure, you'll probably have a pound or two of food left over, but on a trip that short, who cares? Although you can be a bit lackadaisical about quantities, do make an effort to cook only what you can eat. Leftover food should be packed out, not strewn around or buried, where it will corrupt the eating habits of jays and squirrels. Worse yet, burying scraps will also encourage bears to raid your camp.

Although it would be easy to turn our weekend trips into gourmet extravaganzas, Cora and I still prefer to keep our food packing simple. The first day we eat breakfast at home. For lunch, we usually bring cold-cut sandwiches, corn chips, and a few granola bars for snacks. Dinner is a quick-cooking pasta or rice dish fortified with shredded cheese or a can of tuna, chicken, or turkey. Most grocery stores sell packaged pasta and rice dishes that contain their own dried "sauce," or you can take plain pasta or quick-cooking rice and add a package of dried soup mix. We fill in the chinks with a bagel. For dessert, we drink hot chocolate and sometimes split a candy bar. (Okay, I confess, it's a *big* candy bar.) Breakfast the second day (our first one in the field) is always cold cereal with powdered milk. Lunch is a near-repeat of the first day, substituting cheese for cold cuts, which would spoil, and we're home or on the road for dinner.

Backpackers who walk to eat—rather than eat to walk—can find legions of backcountry cookbooks to help them plan more exciting fare. I can recommend two: *Camp Cooking* and *The Trekking Chef*, both from Lyons & Burford.

THREE- AND FOUR-DAY TRIPS

As your adventures grow longer, you must pay increasing attention to exactly how much food you bring. The eyeball method leads to considerable errors when the trip is three or four days or more. Measuring out foods by volume can work if you know how many cups you typically eat for each individual item you want to bring. However, an easier way to bring exactly the right amount is to weigh out your food on a postage scale. I know that 5 ounces of cereal, of any type, and 1 ounce of powdered milk is a satisfying breakfast for me. I have no idea how many cups of my six favorite cereals equal 5 ounces.

Foods differ greatly in their caloric content per ounce. As a general rule, carbohydrates and protein yield about 112 calories per ounce. Fats yield much more: about 250 calories per ounce. Since weight and bulk are a problem while backpacking, it's tempting to load your pack up with fats. Unfortunately, the best food for strenuous exercise consists of carbohydrates, which are relatively heavy for their caloric content. The best backpacking menu, therefore, is a compromise. Think of your food as firewood. Carbohydrates are the kindling, useful for getting the fire going fast and reenergizing a tired hiker quickly. Slow-burning fats and protein are like logs, good for fueling a steadily burning fire and stoking the inner furnaces during a long, cold winter night. Don't worry too much about obtaining sufficient amounts of vitamins and minerals while backpacking. It's impossible to become seriously deficient in any particular nutrient during a week or two of hiking.

Most people need approximately 2 pounds of dry food per person per day. I'm 5'8", 137 pounds, and I find I can get by on a couple of ounces less. Cora, who's smaller than I am, needs a bit less than I do. Here's a prototype menu that Cora and I have used for four-day trips. The quantities listed are merely suggestions to get you in the right ballpark.

FOOD FOR ONE PERSON FOR ONE DAY	
Breakfast	
cold cereal	5 ounces
powdered milk	1 ounce
instant coffee	.25 ounce
nondairy creamer	.5 ounce
Lunch	
bagel or plain crackers	3 ounces
peanut butter or cream cheese	3 ounces
cookies, snack crackers or chips	3 ounces
Dinner	
rice or noodle dish	3 ounces
cheese or canned meat	3 ounces
bagel or plain crackers	3 ounces
cocoa	2 ounces
chocolate candy	2 ounces
TOTAL	**28.75 ounces**

In the summer in the Rockies, fresh bagels and cheese will keep for about three, maybe four days without refrigeration. After that, they become possible sources for exciting new antibiotics. To avoid becoming guinea pigs on the fourth day, we often substitute crackers for the bagel and a small can of meat for the cheese. Sugary foods are easy to bring backpacking, since they're compact and keep well, but Cora and I find that the sweetness becomes sickening if we bring too much, even though we both have a sweet tooth the size of a saber-toothed tiger's. Crunchy foods are often in high demand in the backcountry, which is why we usually bring corn chips or snack crackers. Eventually, of course, these brittle snack items crumble into bird food, but they're still quite palatable if you change your attitude. Simply decide that what you really wanted all along is croutons, and sprinkle them on your pasta or rice. These snacks are bulky, but not heavy in comparison to their caloric content, and they have a side benefit: They make your pack look enormous, which encourages impressionable tourists to make laudatory comments on the trail. (Of course, you have to ignore the scorn of modern-day John Muirs who are out for a week with a pack no bigger than a baguette.)

Some foods suit the backcountry better than others. When I was guiding expeditions on Mt. McKinley, I remember cooking gallons of oatmeal and cream of wheat and seeing a few tablespoons disappear reluctantly into people's mouths. Perhaps the texture began to seem a little too glutinous to stomachs already unsettled by the altitude and enormous exertion. Cold cereal can always be made hot, if so desired, but the opposite is not true. People also quickly rejected excessively fatty food, such as salami, because it upset their stomachs when they began laboring uphill again after lunch. The candy bars everyone scarfed up eagerly during the first few days also became tiresome quickly. One climber commented to me after a week on the glacier, "I don't want to see another Milky Way bar as long as I live." The foods that did retain their appeal were what I call "real food." Cold cereal always tasted good for breakfast. Mildly sweet logan bread for lunch never palled. A bagel, carefully thawed, then buttered, always went down well, as did a dinner glop richly reinforced with cheese and butter.

So far, I've only mentioned foods that are readily available in any well-stocked grocery store. One alternative is to buy freeze-dried food from a backpacking shop or mail-order catalog. Freeze drying is a high-tech method of preserving food that creates a product that can be rehydrated much more satisfactorily than ordinary dehydrated food. Unfortunately, you'll get more pleasure letting the names of the various dishes roll around on your tongue than you will from eating the dishes themselves—and you'll get more pleasure from that than from actually eating the food. Supermarket foods are generally much less expensive than freeze-dried food, and they can be just as tasty. The real key to enjoying backpacking food is variety, not expense. When I was helping guide an expedition on 22,834-foot Aconcagua, the highest peak in the Western Hemisphere, we brought a large number of Alpine Aire freeze-dried dinners because everyone had eaten so many Mountain House dinners on previous trips that they were heartily sick of them. Given a choice at the beginning of the trip, everyone immediately grabbed for the Alpine Aire dinners. After a couple of weeks of Alpine Aire, however, everyone suddenly decided that a Mountain House dinner would be a delectable feast.

Despite all the flack I've given freeze-dried food, I must admit that I brought it for all of my expeditions to Alaska. The reason? Convenience. With most freeze-dried food, you simply add boiling water to the foil pouch and let it sit for five or ten minutes. There's no need to stir the glop to keep it from burning, no pot to clean, and you can be heating the water for your cup of cocoa while you eat your dinner—or, as we always did in Alaska, you can be melting more snow, an interminable task during high-altitude Arctic trips.

FOOD FOR LONG-HAUL BACKPACKING

All of the issues I've discussed above become critical if you're planning a trip lasting a week or longer. For most people, seven to ten days is about as long as they can go before they need to resupply. Even if you could find a pack big enough to carry more days of food, you probably couldn't pick it up without assistance once you filled it, and your shoulders, hips, knees and feet would declare a sit-down strike after the first mile. Even if the trip lasts only a week, bulk can be a major problem. You'll probably find yourself tying cumbersome items of clothing to the outside of your pack and perhaps lashing a bag of food outside as well. I like to lash my rain gear outside because it's usually the item of clothing I need in the biggest hurry.

To help cut down on bulk, shed excess packaging. You'll find that much food as it comes from the grocery store is swaddled in unnecessary amounts of cardboard, foil, and paper. You can reduce

REPACKAGING SINGLE-SERVING PACKETS
OF FOOD INTO ONE PLASTIC BAG CAN SAVE
A LOT OF BULK IN YOUR PACK.

the amount of bulk tremendously by repackaging these items. For example, several companies sell dried soups in individual serving packets. Rip open the packets and put three days' worth in a small plastic bag. You'll be amazed at how compact the bag is compared to the three foil-lined packets. One caveat: be sure to save the cooking directions! Where possible, avoid items packaged as individual servings altogether. Instead, buy the same item in one large, undivided package, then measure it out yourself as needed during the trip. This saves room in the landfill as well as your pack. Cora and I do carry crackers in their cardboard boxes occasionally, since they resist crumbling much longer if carried that way.

LOGAN BREAD

6 eggs
3 cups flour (any mixture of whole wheat and rye)
3/4 cup wheat germ
1/4 cup brown sugar
1/2 cup powdered milk
1 cup oil
1/2 cup honey
1/4 cup molasses
1/4 sorghum syrup or maple syrup
(any combination of these four sweeteners totaling one cup works fine)
1/2 cup shelled walnuts or pecans
1 cup dried fruit (raisins, dates, apricots, peaches, etc.)

HOMEMADE LOGAN BREAD KEEPS WELL AND TASTES GOOD ON THE TRAIL.

Beat all the ingredients together in a large bowl. Pat down into two greased 5 × 9 loaf pans. Bake at 275° for two hours, or until a tester comes out clean. The bread will be very heavy and dense. Each loaf weighs 24 ounces.

94

People hiking the full length of the Appalachian Trail or the Pacific Crest Trail usually recruit a friend to serve as their "ground-control" person, whose job is to ship a box of food at weekly intervals to the towns closest to the hikers' route. Naturally, the hikers should pack each box in advance. Boxes should be left unsealed until the last minute so the ground-control person, perhaps better known as the baggage handler, can add a few fresh items just before sending the box on its way. Boxes should also contain a few other items, like a fresh book, more toilet paper, more sunscreen and lip sunblock, and extra batteries for headlamps and cameras. Long-distance hikers often find that they want to shed some items along the way, such as exposed film, unnecessary items of clothing, maps whose usefulness is past, and guidebooks which led to three wrong turns in three miles. Each box should include tape and padded envelopes and perhaps a cardboard box, broken down flat, so that returning these items is easy. Before the trip, hikers should also gather together some items that may be needed in the event of unforeseen calamities. These items might include spare tent poles, extra first-aid supplies, or extra spare parts for the stove. If required, the ground-control person can include the necessary items in the next shipment.

Food for backpacking will never quite equal the delights you can produce in your own kitchen or the delicacies you can pay restaurateurs to produce in theirs. To remain blissfully content in the backcountry, you need to learn the truth of Lucius Annaeus Seneca's words, written in the first century A.D.: "A great step toward independence is a good-humored stomach, one that is willing to endure rough treatment."

HITTING THE TRAIL

"Until one is committed there is hesitancy,
the chance to draw back, always
ineffectiveness. Concerning all acts of
initiative (and creation), there is one
elementary truth, the ignorance of which
kills countless ideas and splendid plans: that
the moment one definitely commits
oneself, then Providence moves too."

—William H. Murray, *The Scottish Himalayan
Expedition*, 1951

I t didn't seem like an ambitious undertaking when my dad and I decided to hike up Mount Baldy, a 10,000-foot peak in the mountain range ringing Los Angeles. After all, the trail head was quite high, so we wouldn't need to gain much elevation to reach the summit. As we studied the map, we did notice that the trail led over several unnamed subsidiary peaks between the parking lot and the summit, but we dismissed these peaklets as pimples on the elephant's back, too insignificant to slow down an eager teenager and his unsuspecting father.

Ten hours later, with the sun already below the western horizon, the last pimple between our tired bodies and the car had been transformed into a peak of Himalayan proportions. Never again would we neglect to add up *all* the elevation gain along our proposed hike instead of just computing the difference between the starting point and the summit. Each of those "peaklets" had added some 500 feet of elevation gain to both the outbound and the return trips. They had turned what we had thought would be a romp into a late-evening ordeal. By the time we were able to call home and tell my mother we were fine, she was almost ready to alert the search-and-rescue squad.

PLANNING A HIKE

The first step in planning a hiking trip, whether it will take a day or a month, is obtaining topographic maps of the area where you plan to hike. Like most maps, a topo map shows mountains, lakes, streams, roads, trails and other man-made objects. Unlike other maps, however, a topographic map also shows the elevation and shape of the land's peaks and valleys by means of contour lines. These are lines drawn on the map that represent lines of equal elevation on the ground. For an example, look at figure A, which shows Mount Conehead, a mythical cone-shaped peak with contour lines drawn on its surface. Compare figure A to figure B, which shows how the same peak would be represented on a topographic map. Figure C shows an oblique cutaway view of deep, V-shaped Vildernest Valley as it cuts through a level

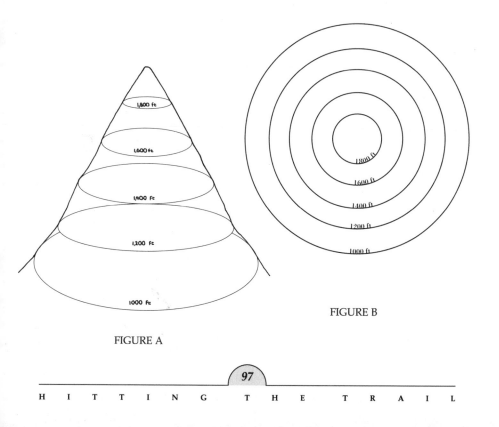

FIGURE B

FIGURE A

FIGURE C

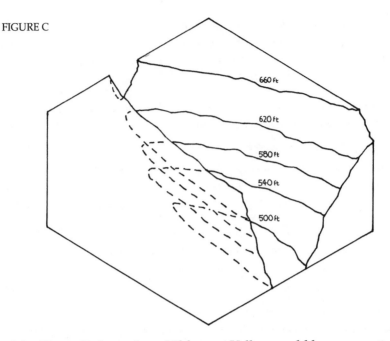

plain. Figure D shows how Vildernest Valley would be represented on a topo map. Figure E shows Bigbeak Peak, a misbegotten mountain with a pronounced ridge jutting out from its summit. Figure F shows how Bigbeak Peak would be represented on a topo map. Note how the soft Vs formed by the contour lines representing a valley in figure D point toward higher elevations, while the Vs formed by the contour lines representing a ridge in figure F point to lower elevations. Use this

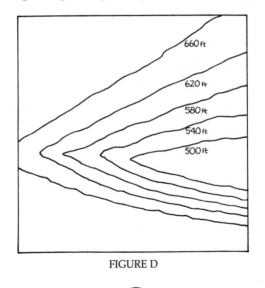

FIGURE D

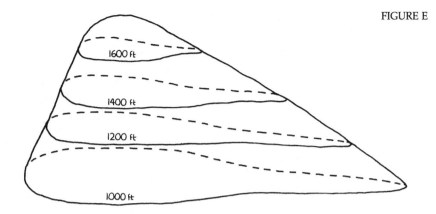

fact to help you distinguish between valleys and ridges on confusing topo maps. The interval between light contour lines is normally 40 or 80 feet. Every fifth contour line is darker. It represents an elevation change of 200 or 400 feet. The contour interval is always stated on the margin of the map.

The U.S. Geological Survey publishes detailed topographic maps covering nearly every area in the United States where you might want to hike. The 15-minute series maps use a scale of one inch to the mile: one inch on the map equals one mile on the ground. Each map covers roughly 240 square miles. These maps have now been mostly replaced by the newer and much more useful 7 1/2-minute series maps, which use a scale of about 2-1/2 inches to the mile. Each map covers roughly 60 square miles. You can obtain USGS maps from many outdoor shops and also by mail. To order by mail, you need to know the name of the map you want and its series. To find that out, write to

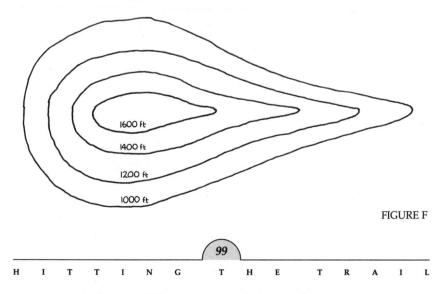

FIGURE F

the USGS at the address in the appendix and request an index for the state you're interested in. The index is actually a large map of the state showing the name and location of each USGS map covering some part of the state. Each index also lists private map dealers in that state.

In the wilderness, paper maps like those from the USGS live a life that's nasty, brutish, and short. A slightly more expensive but much more durable alternative is to buy maps printed on tough, flexible plastic sheets from Trails Illustrated (address in the appendix). Another advantage of the Trails Illustrated topos is that they are updated more frequently than the USGS maps. One disadvantage: the scale is usually one inch to the mile, which makes it harder to decipher fine detail.

Learning to read a topo map by studying a book is like learning to fish in a bathtub. The best way to speed up the learning process is to obtain a map for an area with which you're familiar, then spend time in that area relating the features on the map to the features on the ground. Although reading topo maps quickly and accurately takes a little practice, it's a crucial skill when estimating how long a hike will take.

With a topo map in front of you, you can estimate the length of your proposed adventure. Position one end of a piece of string at the start of your hike; then trace out the trail with the string, being careful to follow all the trail's windings as best you can. When you reach your destination, mark that position on the string with a thumbnail. Now bring the string to the mileage scale on the map's margin. The scale shows how many inches equals a mile. Measure the string with the mileage scale, counting in miles instead of inches, and you'll have a crude estimate of the length of your intended route.

Most trails twist and turn much more than any mapmaker can show. Adding a 10 or 20 percent fudge factor will probably get you closer to reality. (If, on the other hand, you want to convince a reluctant companion just how easy your proposed mountain marathon really is, all you have to do is use an unobtrusively elastic string to trace out the trail. When you bring the string down to the mileage scale to measure it, casually let the string relax and shorten. "See? It's only four miles from the trail head to Mount Inaccessible!")

The next task—the one we neglected on our hike up Mount Baldy—is to estimate the elevation gain and loss along your route. To do this, you need to track the trail carefully as it climbs up and down. Add up each increment of elevation gain and elevation loss to get a true picture of the amount of exertion required.

Most people carrying moderate loads walk about 2 miles an hour on a level trail. Each 1,000 feet of elevation gain adds an hour to that basic estimate; each 1,000 feet of loss adds about half an hour. Rest stops are in addition to these figures. They can add up quickly, so if you're trying to pour on the miles, keep an eye on your watch. Cora and I find that 8 to 10 miles with 2,000 or 2,500 feet of elevation gain when carrying an overnight pack is a full but certainly not overwhelming day. Anything much longer than 12 starts to feel like an Olympic competition; anything less than 6 is a romp. Your own appetite for miles may vary tremendously from ours, depending on fitness, motivation and whether you place greater value on comfort in camp or a light pack on the trail.

There's no need to train for three months before embarking on your first backpacking trip. It's not a marathon. Nonetheless, fitness—or, rather, operating within your level of fitness, whatever it is—will make your trip more enjoyable unless you relish the challenge of pushing yourself beyond your normal limits. One bad health habit—smoking—clearly inhibits your ability to enjoy backpacking, although backpackers, too, will walk a mile for a camel—if it will carry their load the rest of the way.

On occasion I venture into the wilderness by myself, a practice which is correctly discouraged by land managers and search-and-rescue groups. Solo wilderness travel—and particularly solo climbing—has its risks. Even a relatively minor mishap, such as a severely sprained ankle, could turn a Sunday stroll into a survival epic if you happened to be far enough off the trail that no passersby could be expected. However, in the summer, if you stick to well-traveled trails, the added danger of going alone is slight. In the winter, or off-trail at any time of year, the additional danger is real. As a minimal first step toward safety, solo adventurers should tell someone reliable precisely where they are going and when they plan to return.

PACKING YOUR PACK

Once you have selected an itinerary and heaped up everything you want to bring in the middle of your living room, you need to find a way to stuff all of it in your pack. For walking on decent trails, you generally want to put the heaviest gear high in your pack and as close to your spine as possible. That allows you to assume a more comfortable, upright posture because the weight is balanced over your hips. For off-trail scrambling, skiing, and snowshoeing, you still want the heaviest items close to your spine, but you probably want the weight a little lower, to make you less top-heavy. These are general guidelines; as a practical matter, I always pack my pack with the items I'm least likely to need during the day at the bottom, then continue to stow items in ascending order of daytime utility. That means my sleeping bag always goes in first, followed by my extra sweater, stove, fuel, tent, and main bag of food. Lunch goes in the pack's top pocket. I stow my water bottle at the very top of the main compartment or in a side pocket. The only time I've noticed a significant deterioration in the way my pack

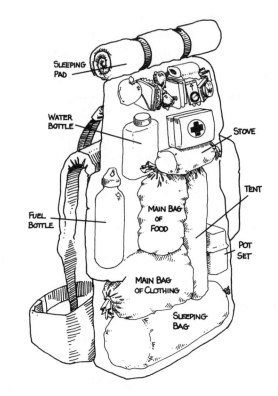

SLEEPING PAD

WATER BOTTLE

STOVE

TENT

FUEL BOTTLE

MAIN BAG OF FOOD

POT SET

MAIN BAG OF CLOTHING

SLEEPING BAG

WHEN PACKING A SINGLE-COMPARTMENT, INTERNAL-FRAME PACK, PUT THE ITEMS YOU'RE LEAST LIKELY TO NEED DURING THE DAY, LIKE YOUR SLEEPING BAG, ON THE BOTTOM.

rode was when I lashed something quite dense and heavy, like a big tripod or heavy tent, to the front or side of the pack. Ideally, items like that should be inside your pack near your spine if you have got an internal frame, or lashed horizontally across the top of the frame near your shoulders if you have got an external frame.

In rainy country, almost every item in your pack should be stowed inside a stuff sack or plastic bag. That way, if it's raining when you unload your pack at camp, you can set things down on the ground without their becoming instantly soaked. Sleeping bags are worth extra care. I often reinforce the water-resistance of the sleeping-bag stuff sack with a plastic bag. The waterproof pack covers sold by some companies don't really solve the problem, since you have to take them off to unload your pack, at which time you'll want everything in stuff sacks or plastic bags anyway.

Some people suggest packing small quantities of liquids you may want, like hand lotion or sunscreen, in film canisters. Beware! I've seen them blow open on several occasions. Better to use little plastic bottles with screw-on tops such as some hotels use to package shampoo for guests. You can also find "travel-size" bottles in well-equipped

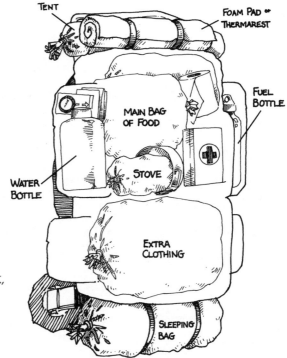

TENT

FOAM PAD or THERMAREST

FUEL BOTTLE

MAIN BAG OF FOOD

WATER BOTTLE

STOVE

EXTRA CLOTHING

SLEEPING BAG

WHEN PACKING AN EXTERNAL-FRAME PACK, LASH YOUR SLEEPING BAG ON THE BOTTOM, BELOW THE PACK BAG, AND AFFIX YOUR TENT AND SLEEPING PAD ON TOP.

drugstores and supermarkets. Sunscreen often comes in squeeze bottles with flip-top lids that tend to pop open and create a problem which remains undiscovered until your entire pack or jacket pocket is coated with slime. I like to tape those flip-top lids shut, then unscrew the whole cap when I need access to the contents.

The easiest way to get a heavy pack on your back is to enlist the aid of a friend who can help hold it up while you slip your arms through the shoulder straps. The second easiest way is to set the pack on a solid support, like a rock, stump, fallen log or tailgate, that's about three feet high. Sit down beside the pack, slip your arms through the straps, and stand up. Lacking a friendly rock or person to help, you'll have to do it yourself. Face the back of the pack, the side with the straps. Loosen each shoulder strap slightly, then grab one shoulder strap with each hand and hoist the pack up onto your bent right knee. Steady the pack there with your left hand and slip your right arm and shoulder through the right-hand shoulder strap. The pack will now be on your back, supported by the right-hand shoulder strap. Slip your left arm through the left shoulder strap, snug down the shoulder straps, fasten and tighten the hip belt, moan and groan a few times to

TO PICK UP A HEAVY PACK, START BY
FACING THE BACK OF THE PACK AND
GRASPING THE SHOULDER STRAPS;
THEN . . .

HOIST THE PACK TO YOUR BENT
RIGHT KNEE . . .

impress your trail companions, and you're set.

Well, almost set. Adjusting your pack is actually a continuous process that most people learn to do while they're walking. Hip belts loosen frequently and need to be retightened. Shoulder stabilizer straps get loose and need to be snugged down. Hips get sore, making it imperative to shift some weight to the shoulders by loosening the hip belt. Then the shoulders get sore, and it's time to cinch down the hip belt again and loosen the shoulder straps. One serious symptom to watch out for is numbness or tingling in your hands, caused by too much weight on your shoulders. If that happens, take the pack off for a few minutes until the tingling eases. When you put it back on, make sure the hip belt is tight enough to carry most of the weight.

ROUTE FINDING

If the trip you've planned goes through heavily traveled back-country, such as that found in many national parks in the summer, then route finding consists primarily of knowing the name of your destination, reading the trail signs, and staying on the trail. As the country gets wilder and more rugged, the trails more obscure or nonexistent, you need to become increasingly savvy about using a map and compass. In the winter in the high mountains, when snow obscures all trails and

PUT YOUR RIGHT ARM THROUGH THE
RIGHT-HAND SHOULDER STRAP . . .

THEN INSERT YOUR LEFT ARM
THROUGH THE LEFT-HAND
SHOULDER STRAP, FASTEN THE HIP
BELT, AND ADJUST ALL STRAPS FOR A
COMFORTABLE FIT.

clouds frequently shroud the peaks, an accurate altimeter is another
highly valuable tool.

A full treatise on the art of backcountry navigation would fill an
entire book of its own. If you'd like to pursue this subject in depth, you
might want to read my book *The Outward Bound Map and Compass
Handbook*, published by Lyons & Burford. What follows is an introduc-
tion to the basics.

The best kind of compass for wilderness navigation is called a
protractor or, more commonly, a baseplate compass. The baseplate is a
rectangular piece of clear plastic. The round capsule mounted on the
baseplate houses the compass needle, which can rotate freely within
the capsule, coming to rest with its north end pointing to magnetic
north. A viscous liquid damps the needle's swing. The capsule is
marked with the 360° that make a full circle. Zero (or 360)° equals
north; 90° equals east; 180° equals south; 270° equals west. The capsule
can be rotated in relation to the baseplate. The index mark on the
baseplate aligns with the edge of the capsule to show you the bearing
(the angle) you've set on the compass. The direction-of-travel arrow is
essentially an extension of the index mark. The gate is a pair of lines (or
sometimes a box) in which you position the north end of the compass
needle when determining directions.

This combination of features allows you to do fancy tricks like taking the bearing of a landmark and measuring a course on the map. I won't get into measuring bearings and courses here since you'll rarely need those skills if you stick to trails. What you do need to know is how to orient the map so that true north on the map corresponds to true north on the ground. To do that, you need to learn how to make the direction-of-travel arrow point to true north.

As most people know, true north and magnetic north do not lie in precisely the same direction. The difference is called the declination. Compass needles point to *magnetic* north. Maps are drawn so that *true* north lies at the top of the map. Stated another way, this means that the right and left edges of the map represent lines running true north and true south. Declination varies from place to place on the earth. Sometimes magnetic north lies to the west of true north; sometimes it lies to the east.

I highly recommend spending a few extra dollars on a "set-and-forget" compass: one that takes care of complex declination calculations for you. With these compasses, the gate can be moved in relation to 0 on the capsule. This lets you set the declination once for your particular place on earth. For example, let's say the declination is 10° east, which means that magnetic north lies 10° to the east of true north. The gate can be set so that it always aligns with the 10° mark on the capsule. Now, when you align the compass needle in the gate and set the capsule so 0 is opposite the index mark, the direction-of-travel arrow will point to true north rather than magnetic north, as shown in figure G.

Orienting the map so that north on the map points in the same direction as north on the ground is simple if you have got a set-and-forget compass. Look on the margin of your topo map, where you'll find the declination for that region. Set the declination on your compass and forget about declination for the rest of your trip. Now set the capsule to 0 and rotate the compass until the needle is within the gate. The direction-of-travel arrow now points to true north. Place the map so that the long edges of the baseplate are parallel to either the right or left edge of the map, and the map is oriented. North on the map equals north on the ground. This also means that a line from your position on the map to a landmark on the map should also point to the same landmark on the ground. (See figure H.)

Orienting your map if you don't have a set-and-forget compass is a tad more complicated. With these conventional compasses, the gate is fixed so that it is always opposite the 0 mark on the capsule. Let's say the declination diagram on your map shows that magnetic north lies 10° to the east of true north. On the capsule, 0 is the same as 360 degrees. Subtract 10° from 360 to get 350. Set the capsule to 350. Orient

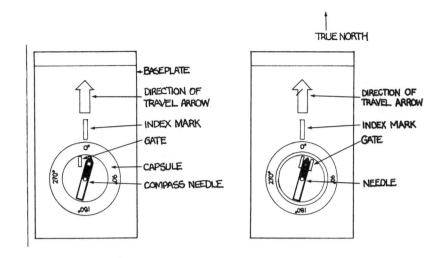

FIGURE G   FIGURE H

the compass so the needle is in the gate. The direction-of-travel arrow will now point to true north, as shown in figure I. Place the map so that the long edges of the baseplate align with either the right or left edge of the map. The map is now oriented correctly. If the declination is 10° west, you would set the capsule to 10° and orient the compass so the needle is in the gate, as shown in figure J. Life gets even more complicated when you're trying to measure bearings and courses with a conventional compass; that is why I recommend set-and-forget compasses so strongly.

You should orient your map for the first time at the trail head, before starting your hike. Study the oriented map, then relate the features marked there to the features in the terrain around you. For example, if there is a big mountain at the head of the valley you'll be hiking

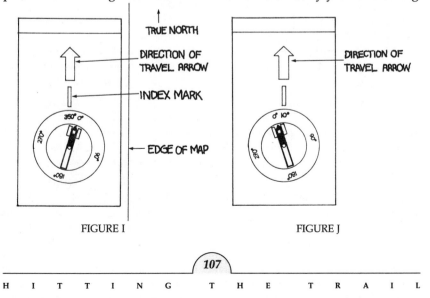

FIGURE I   FIGURE J

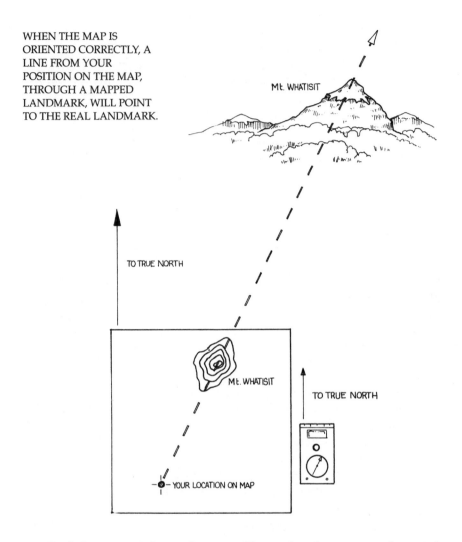

WHEN THE MAP IS
ORIENTED CORRECTLY, A
LINE FROM YOUR
POSITION ON THE MAP,
THROUGH A MAPPED
LANDMARK, WILL POINT
TO THE REAL LANDMARK.

Mt. WHATISIT

TO TRUE NORTH

Mt. WHATISIT

TO TRUE NORTH

— YOUR LOCATION ON MAP

up, find that mountain on the map. Try to develop a general mental picture of the route you'll be following. For example, your route might head north up a river valley, then reach a trail junction just after the second large lake. At the junction, you're supposed to turn west and climb the flanks of the valley to a high pass. If halfway through your hike you've already passed three large lakes and two 7-Elevens and still haven't found the trail junction, something is askew. As you travel, pause periodically to turn around and examine what the terrain will look like during your return trip. You'll find that terrain you have just traveled through can seem quite unfamiliar when you encounter it traveling in the opposite direction. On occasion, during your hike, check the map and compass. Try to keep a general sense of the direction you're traveling. It can be surprisingly easy to get turned around, even for an experienced hiker.

One recent September, Cora and I embarked on a two-day back-packing trip in the Lost Creek Wilderness southwest of Denver. The wilderness derives its name from the astonishing way in which Lost Creek appears out of nowhere, then vanishes into caverns in solid rock walls, only to reappear a quarter of a mile farther downstream. The terrain is rugged and complex, full of granite domes, towers, and buttresses, and the trails corkscrew constantly.

A steady rain set in about noon on our first day, and by dusk we were tired, damp, and ready for camp. We knew that the place where we planned to camp was nearby when we pounded down a steep hill and rejoined Lost Creek just where it emerged from a cave in a cliff. Obviously, the trail continued on the far side; just as obviously, there was no bridge, a fact which should have raised our suspicions, since other stream crossings had been bridged. I remembered that the map showed that we wanted to follow the stream, however, so we gritted our teeth, waded across, and continued along the trail, which paralleled the stream.

Within a few hundred yards, the trail grew faint and overgrown, then vanished into a morass of swift water, dense brush, and giant, slippery boulders. I pulled out the map. As I remembered, the trail was marked as continuing along the stream. Still, something was wrong, and it was too late in the day to try to figure it out then. With our feet squishing in our frigid boots, we walked back to the stream crossing and pitched the tent. Once inside, I pulled out the compass. What I had thought was north was actually south. We had followed the stream in exactly the wrong direction.

In the morning, everything became clear. The trail we had followed down to the stream was simply a well-trampled spur trail leading to a popular campsite. The trail on the far side of the creek was probably made by horsemen trying to reach the excellent campsite where we eventually spent the night. After all, horsemen don't worry about crossing streams without bridges; it's not *their* feet that are getting wet. The trail we wanted had indeed continued along the stream, but in the opposite direction. We had lost it the night before, where it made a hard right 100 yards above the creek and sneaked up a narrow, boulder-strewn defile for 50 yards to avoid a cliff. The spur trail down to the well-worn campsite had been much more obvious, and we had simply followed our noses. The whole experience recrystallized a lesson I thought I'd learned long ago: when the correct route is in doubt, the first thing to do is get out the map *and* the compass.

Another common error traps careless hikers who decide to drop their packs and dash up to some scenic overlook, then forget precisely where they left their gear. On a trip many years ago into Utah's Maze, I encountered a pair of hikers who had dropped their packs to go in search of some petroglyphs. They had set their packs right on the trail and continued up a narrow canyon, undoubtedly assuming that there was no possible way they could miss their packs upon their return. During their descent, however, they had followed the dry river bottom rather than taking the parallel trail up on the stream bank that they'd followed on the way up. By the time I encountered them, they had already walked a good half-mile beyond their packs. Fortunately, I had noted their packs and was able to tell them where they were. If you do choose to leave your pack (or camp) for a short jaunt, make sure you note the landmarks nearby very carefully.

TRICKS OF THE TRAIL

People who have never hiked with a substantial load often pace themselves poorly. They fall into the sprint-and-drop routine, rushing up the mountain for a few hundred yards, then collapsing in a heap, panting. When you're backpacking, particularly at the altitudes common in the Rockies and Sierras, slow and steady wins the race. After all, the backpacker's role model—the tortoise—has its home on its back, too. One study of walking showed that the energy expended doubles with each mile-per-hour increase in speed. To reach your destination without exhausting yourself, slow down until you have adopted a pace you can sustain comfortably for an hour without resting. On really steep grades with heavy loads, particularly at high altitudes, you may want to try the rest step: after each step, let the trailing leg straighten completely and lock your knee for a second or two. This allows your skeleton to support most of your weight while your unweighted leading leg gets a brief rest.

When you do pause to rest, rest completely. Get your pack off and sit down. Try to pause at areas that won't suffer from the use. Rest stops are most effective when they are kept brief because of the way your body gets rid of lactic acid buildup, one cause of muscle fatigue. One researcher found that your body can get rid of about 30 percent of the lactic acid buildup in the first five to seven minutes of rest. In the next fifteen minutes, however, you get rid of only about 5 percent more. Prolonged rests also let the body cool down too much, making it even harder to get back on your feet and start humping that load again.

Walking sticks are most useful in rough terrain or in situations where you can't see your feet, such as while hiking in snow that isn't quite deep enough for snowshoes or skis or while wading across a stream. I like to use an old ski pole because the molded grip is easier to hang onto than the smooth shaft of an ordinary walking stick. I should forewarn you, however, that using a ski pole—even in August—will

USING A WALKING STICK AND HOLDING
HANDS WITH A COMPANION CAN HELP
STEADY YOU DURING DIFFICULT STREAM
CROSSINGS.

prompt knucklehead comedians to exclaim, "You forgot your skis!"

Nearly all stream crossings in popular wilderness areas are
bridged these days, but it's still useful to know how to cross a stream
that isn't. The first tactic is to look for a natural bridge: a fallen log.
Depending on the ruggedness of the terrain and the difficulty of fording, it may be worth searching upstream and downstream for a quarter
of a mile to try to find a suitable log. Don't feel compelled to emulate
the Flying Wallendas by walking across the log if it's too narrow or too
high for comfort. There's no shame in straddling the log and working
your way across inch by inch.

If the search for a log proves futile, conquer your natural inclina-
tion to cross at the narrowest point in hopes of spending as little time as
possible in the stream. Narrow means deep, and deep means a good
chance that you'll be swept off your feet if the current is strong and the
water comes up over your knees. Instead, look for a wide spot in the
stream where the water is as shallow as possible. Don't cross right
above a waterfall or rapid. Loosen your shoulder straps, undo your
sternum strap, and loosen or completely unhook your hip belt so you
can shed your pack in a hurry if you do get swept off your feet.
Focusing your eyes on the far bank rather than the rushing water will
help you keep your balance. If the terrain permits, cross downstream
diagonally rather than crossing along a line directly perpendicular to
the banks. You'll waste less strength fighting the current. Make sure

each foot is firmly planted before moving the next. Sometimes it's best to shuffle your feet without crossing your legs. It can also be helpful for two people to link hands to help support each other. Unless the water is clear and the bottom is uniformly sandy, it's best to wear your boots while fording to protect your feet. Wear your boots without your socks while crossing; then put your socks back on before you resume hiking. After your socks have absorbed some of the moisture from the boots, exchange them for dry ones and hang the damp ones off the back of your pack to air-dry. This procedure will help your boots dry as fast as possible and reduce the chance of blisters. It's easy for the inexperienced hiker to underestimate the difficulty of fording a stream. When in doubt, turn back.

Large, late-lingering snowfields that obscure portions of the trail are another possible hazard in spring and early summer in the West's higher regions. In the early morning, such snowfields can be frozen ice-hard, and be just as slippery. Even mountaineers equipped with ice axes, which supposedly give them the ability to stop a slip while snow climbing, have often discovered at great cost how easy it is to slip, fail to catch themselves, and immediately accelerate out of control on steep snow. Usually snowfields that obscure trails will have a deep, rutted path pounded into them by hikers who cross after the snow softens in the midday sun. Following the beaten path can be safe at any time. Danger arises, however, when unwary hikers venture off the path onto steep snow when the snow is frozen hard.

After the snow melts, steep mountain slopes present a different hazard: rockfall. In regions where the rock is naturally rotten, rockfall frequently occurs spontaneously, particularly during a hard rain or when the sun melts the frost holding shattered cliffs and gully walls together. A bigger threat, even in regions where the rock is basically sound, is hikers dislodging stones that then tumble onto hikers below them. In loose terrain, hikers should never travel with one person directly above another. If a gully is too narrow to permit side-by-side travel, one person should move at a time, with the others waiting in a safe place.

The slickrock canyons of the desert Southwest hold danger of a different sort. Sooner or later, all novice hikers make the unpleasant discovery that it's much easier to climb up something than it is to climb down it. The deceptively easy-looking slabs, buttes, and spires that abound in the Southwest have tempted many an unwary hiker into an attempt to scale them. The rock seems so low-angled; beginners don't know that what really makes rock difficult to climb is not steepness, but lack of holds, a characteristic for which sandstone is notorious. If you are tempted to scramble up something, go up just 10 feet, then turn around and come back down. If descending is completely comfortable, then it may be reasonable to continue upward cautiously if the rock becomes no more difficult. Just remember that every step up will have to be reversed, and that a slip even 20 or 30 feet off the ground can easily be fatal.

TRAIL ETIQUETTE

One beautiful July day when Cora and I were hiking in the Indian Peaks Wilderness, we came across a lush field of flowers sprawling across a steep hillside. The trail cut right across the hillside, directly through the flower patch, but it was obvious to me that the best vantage point for a photograph was about 30 feet below the trail. I examined the area carefully and finally selected a circuitous route to my vantage point that allowed me to avoid trampling any flowers. No sooner had I made my picture, returned to the trail and continued onward, however, when I overheard a couple arguing behind me. "Stay on the trail!" the woman scolded her boyfriend, who was about to follow in my footsteps to make his own photograph. "But *he* did it!" the man replied, obviously referring to me.

Immediately I realized that I had made a mistake. The slope I had descended to reach my photo op was steep and unstable. Although I had watched my footing carefully, I had undoubtedly disturbed the soil and the low-lying plants as I edged my boot soles into the slope to avoid slipping. In addition to the damage I had done, I'd set a very bad example—an example that had almost been followed immediately. Regardless of how careful subsequent photo maniacs had been, the fragile vegetation holding the highly erodible soil in place would inevitably have been injured. Once it died, erosion would have begun. Snowmelt and summer rains would have stripped away what little topsoil existed in that harsh alpine environment. Within a summer or two that flower field, which had delighted thousands of visitors every summer for decades, would have disappeared, leaving behind an ugly scar.

The first rule of trail etiquette is simple: stay on the trail. The more heavily used the wilderness and the more fragile the landscape, the greater the importance of this rule. Some beauty spots, like that flower field, should be treated like works of art. Few people are so boorish that they would trample across a painting if it were laid out on the ground in front of them. Alpine meadows should be treated with equal respect.

Staying on the trail also means refraining from cutting switchbacks, the places where a trail makes a hairpin turn and almost doubles back on itself. It's tempting to the ill-informed to leave the trail just before the turn and take a "shortcut," regaining the trail just after the turn. This, too, is an invitation to severe erosion, which, once started, is extremely difficult to stop. For the same reason, you should avoid walking side by side on a trail unless it was built to accommodate such traffic. Few trails are. Walking side by side will widen the trail and, if it crosses a steep slope, tend to break down the outside of the tread—the level portion of the trail where you walk—causing the trail itself to deteriorate. Whenever possible, avoid walking around mud holes that form in low spots on the trail. This practice turns narrow wilderness paths into highways as hikers' boots trample and kill the trailside vegetation. Instead, buy yourself a pair of waterproof boots and charge ahead fearlessly. You may find it gives you a perverse pleasure as it reminds you of your childhood when you went stomping through the puddles, throwing a glorious spray of water in all directions and greatly annoying your mother. In any case, mud will fall off your boots faster than vegetation will grow back. Treat little snow patches on the trail the same as mud holes: blast on through the snow rather than walking around and killing the vegetation to the side of the trail. During early summer hikes, when snow patches are frequent, you'll probably want to wear gaiters to keep the snow out of your boots.

The meaning of "staying on the trail" can be quite difficult to decipher when you suddenly find yourself confronted by three trails—all running parallel to each other—about a foot apart. Multiple trails frequently begin when fussy hikers with porous footwear walk alongside a muddy trail rather than directly on it. In other places, multiple trails begin when the original trail has been built with too-few water bars, the low wooden or stone barriers across a trail that divert flowing water off the tread. Without sufficient water bars, the trail itself becomes a stream during the spring runoff. Soon the trail erodes into a foot-deep, narrow slit choked with boulders. Even when dry, such a mangled trail offers only difficult walking, so thoughtless hikers begin a new trail paralleling the old. I've seen "trails" in rainy Scotland that could have accommodated a truck towing a double-wide trailer. A ranger once described to me a trail in Touloumne Meadows, near Yosemite, that was six lanes wide. The best solution when you're confronted with multiple trails is to pick the one that seems most used and stay with it as much as possible. To be part of the long-term solution, consider volunteering on a trail-maintenance crew. Many local conservation organizations organize such crews each summer. Federal land managers can often tell you which group is doing what.

There are a few exceptions to the stay-on-the-trail rule. The most common involves horses. Hikers should yield the right-of-way to horses by walking a few feet off the trail and standing quietly while the horses pass by. Hikers traveling downhill should also yield to hikers laboring uphill. After all, they're working harder than you are.

As you gain more experience, you may find situations where

you want to leave the trail behind completely and take off cross-country. In many parts of the nation, the alpine tundra above timberline provides easy walking and breathtaking 360° views. Unfortunately, it's not always environmentally acceptable to succumb to the off-trail urge. In the White Mountains of New Hampshire, for example, rangers urge all hikers to stay on the trail at all times. There are simply too many people, and the land is too fragile. In Rocky Mountain National Park, short footpaths lead from heavily traveled Trail Ridge Road across the alpine tundra to scenic overlooks. Signs there urge visitors to stay on the paved footpaths rather than wander off across the easily damaged tundra. In another part of the park, however, off-trail tundra walking is permitted, simply because the people pressure is far lower. In that part of the park, hikers have to follow a steep trail for a couple of miles to reach timberline. As always, the need to flex a little shoe leather quickly discourages the masses of people. When in doubt about the environmental acceptability of a cross-country hike, ask a ranger.

If you're walking off-trail with friends in places where there's no sign of previous passage, your group should spread out to avoid walking in each other's tracks. This minimizes the possibility that your passage will create the beginnings of a herd trail, which other hikers are likely to find and follow. Try to walk through areas that can tolerate the traffic: sandy areas, slickrock and granite benches, talus and scree fields, lingering snowfields. On the alpine tundra in parts of Rocky Mountain National Park, for example, boulders stud broad areas of alpine grass dotted with tiny wildflowers no bigger than a thumbtack. Try to hop from rock to rock as much as possible to avoid trampling the vegetation. Avoid marshy areas where your boots will compact the porous, waterlogged soil. You should also avoid steep slopes where you will have to dig in your toes on the way up and heels on the way down. Your footsteps can start a slope on the path to erosion. Yosemite has a regulation limiting groups to fifteen people if they stay on the trail, but limiting groups to eight if they plan to travel more than a quarter-mile off the trail. This sensible regulation should be adopted by large groups everywhere.

On occasion, you will face a dilemma while hiking off-trail. You come across an incipient trail. Do you use it to confine your impact to already-disturbed ground, or avoid it, hoping it will heal? If a durable route aside from the incipient trail exists (a granite bench or a sandy wash, for example), then take it. Otherwise, use your best judgment, balancing the fragility of the land around the trail with the degree of damage already done.

At times when you are hiking off-trail you may be tempted to build a few cairns (small piles of rocks) to guide you on your return

TRAINING FOR BACKPACKING

We've all met people who punish their bodies ruthlessly with heinous workouts, then proceed to brag insufferably about their accomplishments as they sip Perrier at the party. Fortunately, there's no need to goose-step up the trail with military precision. You will enjoy backpacking more, however, if you make some effort to get in shape before the season begins, then continue a regular exercise program in between trips.

Aerobic fitness, the kind most important for backpacking, is defined as the ability to take in, transport and utilize oxygen. One of the best measures of aerobic fitness, then, is the maximum amount of oxygen you can take in and use per minute. Since heavier people use more oxygen, maximum oxygen uptake is usually expressed in milliliters of oxygen consumed per kilogram of body weight per minute, or ml/kg/min. To estimate your maximum oxygen uptake, run as far as possible in 15 minutes. Record the distance run in meters (1 mile equals 1609 meters). Running on a track of known circumference makes estimating the distance easy. Divide the distance in meters by 15 to find speed in meters per minute. Your maximum oxygen uptake is approximately:

$$MaxVO_2 = [(\text{speed in meters per minute minus } 133) \times .172] + 33.3$$

Minimally fit people score around 40. Champion endurance athletes score in the 70s and 80s.

Sports that guarantee a high sustained heart rate are the best preparation for backpacking. Hiking, cycling, cross-country skiing, and running, particularly over hilly terrain, are all excellent because they train not only the heart and lungs, but also those muscles that will be taxed most heavily on the trail. Swimming, while great for the heart and lungs, should be supplemented by training that works the legs in ways similar to backpacking. Intermittently strenuous sports like tennis and

trip. In general, you should refrain. Instead, learn to memorize landmarks, both large and small. Make a careful mental note of that odd-shaped boulder that marks the correct gully for your descent off the ridge crest. Master a few additional map-and-compass skills so you can shoot a bearing to follow if a whiteout blows in. Turn around frequently and study the terrain as it will look during the trip home. If you absolutely must build a few cairns for safety's sake, be sure to racquetball are good only if played hard enough so that the heart rate goes up and stays up for the entire game.

Everyone has a "training threshold," the minimum intensity and duration of training that stimulates their body to adapt. The more slack your body, the lower your training threshold. The more conditioned your body, the higher the threshold. To keep making progress, increases in the intensity and duration of your training are essential. Brian J. Sharkey, author of *Physiology of Fitness*, gives this rule of thumb for estimating your training zone, the range of heart rates that will produce a training effect. The lower limit is:

Heart rate = 55% (max heart rate − resting heart rate) + resting heart rate.

The upper limit is:

Heart rate = 70% (max heart rate − resting heart rate) + resting heart rate

Your maximum heart rate is about 220 minus your age. To determine your exercise heart rate, take your pulse for 10 seconds immediately after you stop exercising. Sense your pulse with your fingertips at either your wrist or at the carotid artery in your neck just below the point of your jaw. Then multiply by six to get beats per minute. For a 25-year-old with a resting heart rate of 70, the training zone ranges approximately from 140 to 160 beats per minute.

If you are in poor condition now, a workout lasting only 15 minutes may be enough to nudge your body over the training threshold. As you get more fit, extend the workouts until you can train comfortably for 45 minutes to an hour or more. Working out every other day is the minimum for making significant progress. Using an intense burst of effort for about 1/20th of the workout (for example, by picking up the pace for the last quarter-mile of a five-mile run), gives the heart and lungs a useful added training stimulus. To keep track of your progress, record your workouts in a training log.

restore the area to its natural appearance by dismantling them during your return trip.

Trail etiquette includes a few other pointers, some of which are backed up by actual regulations. Pets are usually prohibited in the backcountry in national parks, as are weapons of any sort. Harassing wildlife is also prohibited. Enjoy animals from a distance. If you want to photograph them, buy a long lens (300mm or longer) or content

FOLDING MAPS

Paper maps are rather fragile things, so I like to carry them inside a one-gallon Ziploc bag along with my compass and altimeter. Unfortunately, folding a standard USGS 7 1/2 minute quad into quarters produces a folded map that's slightly too big to fit a one-gallon Ziploc. A slightly more sophisticated method is necessary. Whatever method you choose, use it consistently. Nothing destroys a map faster than folding it repeatedly in different ways.

To use the method I like, start with the map face up with north at the top—the same position you'd use if you just wanted to read it. Bring the top edge down to the bottom edge with the printed side inside, as shown in the diagram, and crease the fold. Now bring the top edge back up to the middle crease, this time with the printed side out. Bring the bottom edge up to the middle crease in the same way, again with the printed side facing out. Now bring the left edge to the right edge. Finally, bring the left edge back to the middle. Do the same with the right edge. The folded map will have its name visible in the upper-right-corner and will fit easily into a one-gallon Ziploc. I store my folded maps upright in a shoebox in alphabetical order with cardboard dividers indicating groups of letters (A-D, E-G, H-L, etc.).

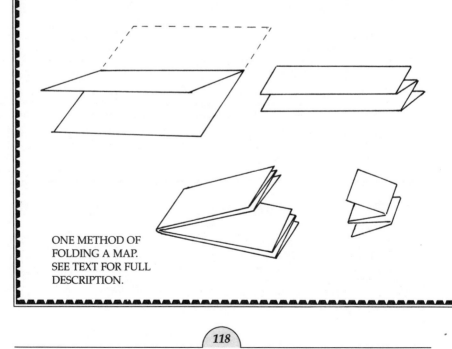

ONE METHOD OF
FOLDING A MAP.
SEE TEXT FOR FULL
DESCRIPTION.

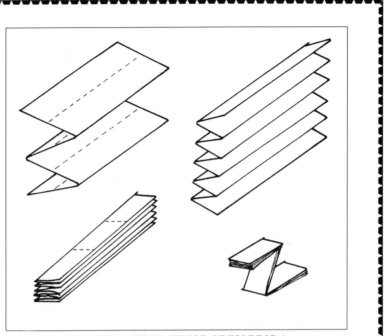

AN ALTERNATIVE METHOD OF FOLDING A
MAP. SEE TEXT FOR FULL DESCRIPTION.

An alternative is the accordion fold. Start as before, with the map's printed side facing up. Bring the right edge to the left edge, (printed side inside), make a sharp crease, then unfold the map flat again, as shown in the illustration. Now bring the right edge to the center, making a quarter-fold. Fold the right edge back to the righthand outermost edge of the folded map, making an eighth-fold. Use these folds as a guide to continue folding until you have eight accordionlike folds. Now fold the map in Z-like thirds, as shown. With this technique, you can look at any part of the map without unfolding the entire sheet.

TRACKING YOUR POSITION IN A DESERT CANYON

Conventional techniques can be nearly useless when you are trying to track your location in one of the Southwest's steep-walled sandstone canyons. The vertical walls usually block your view of nearby landmarks, and the canyon itself may lack features that can be clearly identified on the map. The secret is to start using your map and compass at the very beginning of the trip. The best clue to your location is the direction the canyon is heading. As you enter the canyon, orient your map. In this situation, I like to carry the map and compass in my hand as I walk, referring to it every few hundred yards. Mark your position on the map with your thumbnail and continue along the canyon. Let's say the canyon starts out heading north, then bends to the east. If you keep your map oriented as you hike, you'll notice immediately when the canyon begins its bend and you begin traveling east. Move your thumbnail to your new position. Continue in this way, tracking each twist and turn of the canyon until you reach your destination. Such careful route-finding may be unnecessary if you are planning to do an out-and-back hike with no particular turn-around point in mind. However, if you are searching for a particular side-canyon or petroglyph, or are attempting a loop that requires you to exit the canyon at a particular point, this method is invaluable.

yourself with composing a landscape photograph with the animal as part of the scenery. Feeding animals is also prohibited. Handing out tidbits corrupts the animals' normal eating habits and increases the population artificially, beyond what the land can support in the off-season when all the tourists are gone. In wilderness areas and national parks, every facet of the land is protected. That means that visitors shouldn't pick the flowers. It also means leaving antlers, bones, wind-sculpted driftwood, and all historic and prehistoric artifacts in place. This includes pot shards and arrowheads as well as other objects. Ralph Waldo Emerson expressed this well in 1846:

> "I wiped away the weeds and foam,
> I fetched my sea-born treasures home;
> But the poor, unsightly, noisome things
> Had left their beauty on the shore,
> With the sun and the sand and the wild uproar."

CLEAN CAMPING 101

> "A man is rich in proportion to the number
> of things which he can afford to let alone."
>
> —**Henry Thoreau**, *Walden*

So now you've honed your map-and-compass skills and broken in your new hiking boots on several day-hikes. You're ready for your first overnight trip. Can you just load up your magic pack that's "guaranteed to make weight vanish," and sally forth into the wild green yonder? Not quite.

First you have to get a permit. It's frustrating, but it's a necessity, at least at most of the popular destinations. There are just too many of us who love the wilderness. The backcountry is fragile, given the hordes of people who want to use it. Most national parks began requiring backcountry permits in the late 1960s or early 1970s, as the backpacking boom went ballistic and the damage caused by unregulated camping became apparent. Backpackers quite naturally picked the most beautiful spots to camp: the meadow with a view of the lake, the stream bank beside the joyous brook, the tundra just above the timberline with an incredible view of snow-crowned peaks. And if only a few people per summer had camped in those locations, the damage might have been tolerable. But the number of backpackers grew exponentially. In 1977, the peak year of the boom in many parks, backpackers spent at least 60,000 user-nights (one person for one night) in

Shenandoah National Park and another 102,000 user-nights in Great Smoky Mountains National Park just to the south. Rocky Mountain National Park saw 62,700 user-nights. Yosemite peaked in 1975 with 219,000 user-nights. All told, the national parks recorded about 2.5 million backcountry user-nights in 1977. Waterproof tent floors smothered meadow grasses, streamside vegetation, and alpine tundra. The endless tramp of booted feet compacted the soil around these camps until the soil actually died. Air is vital to the billions of organisms that inhabit the soil. As the soil's porous structure collapsed, so did the soil's ability to support life. The only crop that thrived was fire rings, which sprouted everywhere. The heat of the fires sterilized the soil; the fire itself blackened the rocks with charcoal that would last for thousands of years. As downed wood became scarce, hikers broke, chopped, and sawed dead limbs off trees, then live limbs, scarring the trees permanently. In a misguided effort to save a few ounces on the hike out, backpackers buried their trash or tried to burn it. Too often fire rings became trash pits as well. Toilet-paper flowers flourished as hikers failed to adequately bury their wastes. In the Indian Peaks Wilderness near Denver, camping pressure and destruction grew so great that the valleys leading away from the most popular trail heads were closed to all camping from May 1 to November 30. The only time you can camp there now is when a thick blanket of snow protects the fragile landscape. Similar problems forced park managers to impose restrictions in many other areas.

The number of backpackers declined in the early 1980s, then began climbing again in many areas as the 80s waned and the 90s began. Land managers in most areas feel, with good reason, that restrictions are still necessary. Some areas, like Rocky Mountain National Park, use a designated-site system for the most popular destinations. Backpackers are required to camp in a specified site marked by a stake in the ground. Sites can be reserved. Popular sites are booked up months in advance, but, so far, the backcountry has never become completely full. In addition to the reserved sites, Rocky Mountain National Park also has 23 cross-country zones, all below the timberline, which have no trails and no designated campsites. Hikers can camp anywhere they want within those zones, constrained only by the low-impact camping guidelines and a time limit of one or two nights per zone, no more than one night per camp.

In Yosemite, pressure on the backcountry is controlled by using a quota system limiting the number of backpackers who can start in from each trail head in one day. Half of the available slots can be reserved; the others are available on a first-come, first-served basis. The quotas for the popular trail heads fill up quickly, but there has not yet been a time when the entire backcountry was sold out. After obtaining a permit, backpackers can camp anywhere they choose, again within the constraints imposed by low-impact camping practices. The park strongly recommends that people camp in places where others have camped before on the theory that the damage has already been done. Why ruin a new site as well? Given the high altitude of the Sierras, where vegetation regenerates slowly, such a policy makes sense.

In Shenandoah National Park, by contrast, low-impact camping means seeking out an apparently untouched site that neither day-hikers nor fellow backpackers can see. In the well-watered, low-altitude Blue Ridge Mountains of Virginia, vegetation grows quickly. A stay of one or two nights in an untouched site does little harm. Stays longer than two nights in one site are prohibited. If an area deteriorates, park rangers erect a no-camping sign so the area can recover.

Permits are usually free. You can obtain a permit in person, or, sometimes, by mail, but rarely by phone. For popular parks like Rocky Mountain, Grand Canyon, and Yosemite, and particularly for popular destinations within those parks, plan as far ahead as you can—months ahead, if possible. Some areas limit how far ahead of time you can make a reservation. Permits are usually required year-round, but winter use in mountain areas is often low enough that regulations are relaxed.

As you can see, minimizing your impact on the wilderness can mean different things in different places. One principle, however, is a constant: abide by whatever regulations land managers have applied to the wilderness. For the most part, these regulations have been developed by backcountry rangers who spend a lot more time in the backcountry—and see its problems more often—than you and I. If some regulation seems onerous or unnecessary, write a letter to the backcountry office or park superintendent after you get home. Don't flout the regulations in the backcountry. Experience will soon teach you that nearly all the regulations, as obnoxious as they may at first appear, actually enhance your enjoyment of the wilderness by helping keep it clean, untrammeled and relatively uncrowded.

SELECTING A CAMPSITE

Camping in a designated site is like pulling into slot 76 at the KOA: no thought required. If camping is not restricted to designated sites, then choosing a site requires a great deal more effort. Consider the land before shrugging off your pack with a weary groan and pitching your tent on the first patch of semilevel ground that's not a mine field of anthills and horse manure. Most popular backpacking areas are pockmarked with sites that have already seen intensive use. If a previously used site in an environmentally sound location is available, use it again to confine your impact to as small an area as possible. However, meadows and areas that are wetlands in the spring, even if they are almost dry in late summer, are always off-limits even if someone has camped there before. Catalog pictures and magazine ads that show tents in lush—meaning wet—meadows are trumpeting a lie and encouraging abusive practices that should never be tolerated. Let those sites recover. The same goes for stream and lake banks. Try to camp at least 200 feet from water, even if the regulations permit you to camp closer. By maintaining your distance, you'll spare the vegetation along the bank and ensure that animals can come for a drink without intimidation. Desert bighorn, in particular, will shy away from waterholes if you camp nearby. Avoid camping in the beauty spots, the scenic overlooks and spots with climactic vistas across the lake or up the valley that will certainly draw other visitors. Relish the view from these spots for as long as you want, but don't camp there.

The alpine tundra above the timberline is another highly fragile area. Plants there must endure severe cold, an extremely short growing season, powerful winter storms and the desiccating effect of near-constant wind. Give those plants a chance. Wind and weather also besiege the highest timberline trees, the hardy survivors in the last outpost of the forest empire. Admire their tenacity, but don't stress it further by camping among them. Camping near the timberline or above also puts you in danger from lightning storms, which are frequent in most mountainous areas from late spring to early fall.

In high desert areas, avoid camping or even walking on the dark, knobby crusts of cryptogamic soil that carpet some regions. This crust, a symbiotic association of fungi, moss and cyanobacteria, is literally the glue that holds the soil together, helping prevent erosion when rare but powerful thunderstorms pound the desert. The crust is extremely fragile and takes 50 to 100 years to fully regenerate if it is crushed beneath a careless foot. According to some biologists, microbial crusts similar to cryptogamic soil may well have been the first colonizers of land when life emerged from the sea as much as 3 billion years ago. Those microbes, in turn, may have accelerated the weathering of rock into soil, a process which removed carbon dioxide from the atmosphere. That may have reduced the strength of the greenhouse effect and lowered the Earth's temperature by as much as 54°, making the land much more hospitable to the development of more complex forms of life—such as, eventually, you and me. So don't even *think* of walking on the cryptogam, much less camp on it.

The best sites in forested regions are usually deep in the woods, well away from lakes and streams and out of sight of trails and other campers. Look for areas where pine needle duff or deciduous leaves—not grass—carpet the forest floor and where your tent will not crush any low-growing plants. Beware of standing dead trees or large dead

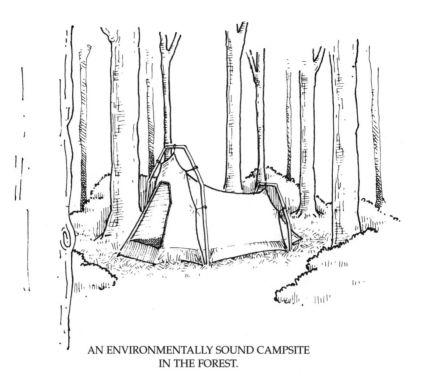

AN ENVIRONMENTALLY SOUND CAMPSITE
IN THE FOREST.

limbs that could topple or break off in a storm and flatten your tent. In some areas, the vegetation in dry meadows and grassy areas is resistant enough to tolerate one night (and one night only) of low-impact use. Such sites are highly visible to both wildlife and other campers, so they are best avoided in most situations.

The best site in the desert is often a level slickrock bench. Sand in your clothes, your hair, your food, and your camera is the bane of desert camping. Camping on slickrock gives you a place to lay down your gear, and yourself, where sand will not immediately infiltrate everything. Lacking a convenient slickrock campsite, grit your teeth (you'll soon be grinding them regardless), and look for regions that don't support vegetation—which means sites graced with sand or gravel. Camping in a sandy wash is tempting because such sites have very little impact, in part because there's no vegetation to harm, and in part because the infrequent rainstorm big enough to cause water to flow in the wash will remove any sign of your camp. Of course, if you happen to be there when the flood descends, it might wash you away, too. Even if it's clear overhead, a thunderstorm upstream can create a dangerous flash flood that wipes out your camp. Resist temptation. Don't camp in the bottom of a wash.

The best sites are found, not made. Save your engineering for winter, when there's four feet of snow on the ground. Don't level sites or "improve" them by digging trenches around your tent to drain away rainwater. Trenches promote erosion, which eventually creates gullies. Refrain from building windbreaks or benches from stones or logs. The archaic practice of cutting pine-bough beds that some turn-of-the-century woodcraft manuals recommended should be relegated to the history books. Try to remember that you're spending a night, not founding a settlement. The longer your stay, the more your campsite will begin to look like the beginnings of a city. If you've camped in a pristine spot, move on after one night.

If you are camped in a previously used site with an established path to water, use the path. If no such path exists, avoid making one. That's easier to do if you can avoid making multiple trips to your water source by bringing an extra water bottle or two, or perhaps a large collapsible water jug if you're traveling in a large group, then filling all your water containers in one trip to the stream or lake. Multiple trips over the same route soon create a visible herd path that encourages more people to walk the same route. If multiple trips are necessary, choose a different route each time to spread out the impact so thinly that no one will notice. Wherever your site, consider bringing a pair of lightweight sneakers or sandals to wear around camp to help reduce your impact on the vegetation. Think of it as evening out the odds in the confrontation between your massive waffle-stompers and the frag-

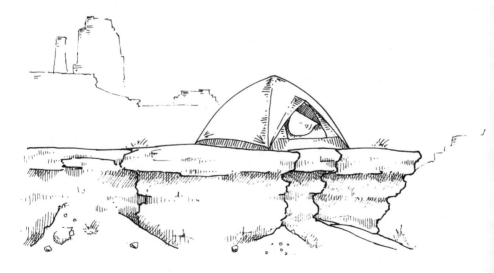

AN ENVIRONMENTALLY SOUND CAMPSITE
ON A SLICKROCK BENCH IN THE DESERT.

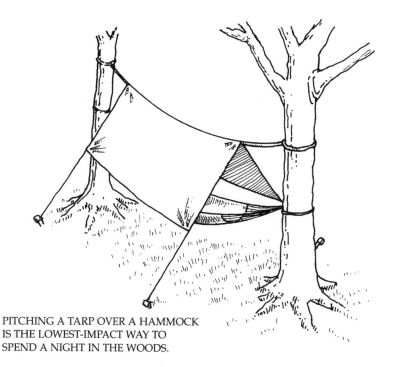

PITCHING A TARP OVER A HAMMOCK
IS THE LOWEST-IMPACT WAY TO
SPEND A NIGHT IN THE WOODS.

ile vegetation. (Okay, in cactus country, the odds are pretty even to begin with.) The goal should be to leave your camp so undisturbed that a visitor the next day would think no one had ever camped there. You do yourself a favor as well as the next visitor by leaving an immaculate camp. Backcountry rangers monitor the damage to the backcountry. If the land suffers, so do you, because the result will be shrinking quotas.

Large groups must take extra care in their selection and use of sites because the potential for damage from such concentrated use is high. Many parks limit group size, so inquire in advance. In the Great Gulf Wilderness in New Hampshire's White Mountains, for example, the group limit is 10. In Yosemite, it's 15. In Mt. Rainier National Park, it's 5 unless you reserve a group site.

At times, you'll face a dilemma in whether to use a slightly worn site or not. If you think there's a chance it will recover, based on your estimate of the amount of damage that's already occurred and the probability of other parties using it in the near future, then it's probably best to leave it alone and camp in a pristine site. If it's already over the edge, and looks as if vegetation won't be able to regrow in the compacted soil, then it's probably best to confine your impact to that one site.

The real gurus of low-impact camping use a sleeping setup that rivals, in its concern for earthly life, the Jain practice of sweeping the

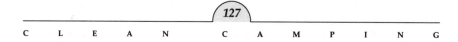

ground ahead of them as they walk for fear of crushing an insect. Their solution? Sleeping in a hammock slung between two trees. Surely no lower-impact way of spending a night in the woods could be devised. A simple plastic or nylon tarp draped over a cord tied between those same trees and staked out at the four corners serves to deflect rain and provide a dry, sheltered nook for cooking in inclement weather. Alas, that tarp cannot serve to deflect mosquitoes, blackflies, deerflies, no-see-ums and other assorted nasties whose collective assault on sanity is the prime reason I rarely go camping without a tent. Although winter in the mountains is too harsh for hammock camping and deserts often lack suitable trees, in the right time and place, a hammock and tarp might well be a lightweight way to practice the low-impact art.

CAMPFIRES

Campfires and the outdoor life have been connected in a deep and visceral way ever since the days when there was no "outdoors" because there was no "indoors" with which to contrast it. Unfortunately, campfires are now like pine-bough beds, lakeside campsites, and four-wheeled brontosaurs that get 10 miles to the gallon: a luxury that we can no longer afford. First, fire rings are an ugly and extremely long-lived reminder that people have passed that way before. Blackened rocks remain discolored for hundreds—if not thousands—of years. That same soot will blacken your pots, which will, in turn, stain everything they touch. Often, mistakenly, people believe their fire will burn almost anything, including food scraps and their trash with its plastic and aluminum foil components. When the fire fails to consume those items, they're often simply left behind, which converts the fire ring into a trash pit for rodents and birds to scavenge. Wood smoke will penetrate your clothes and give them a lingering odor, which may make you feel like Daniel Boone in the backcountry, but will make you smell like a Neanderthal in the city.

In addition, wood smoke is a health hazard. Evidence is growing that inhaling wood smoke leads to reductions in lung function and increased susceptibility to lower-respiratory diseases. Other research has linked compounds in smoke to cancer, heart disease, and central nervous system disorders. One study in the late 1980s showed that 25 percent of Denver's infamous brown cloud was caused by wood smoke. Many mountain towns have enacted restrictions on wood burning to preserve air quality. Murphy's first law of fire-building states that no matter where you sit in relation to your fire, the wind will always shift and blow the smoke in your face. Why expose yourself to the risk? Why contribute, in even a small way, to degrading the quality of wilderness air? Traveling to the wilderness only to build a fire reminds me of the billboard I saw outside Santiago, Chile, a city choking on filthy air caused by millions of automobiles. The billboard, erected by the local Chevy dealer alongside a major highway leading from Santiago to the Andes, showed two children in a car driven by their father. The sign read, "Thank you, Daddy, for taking us to breathe clean air."

Fire building causes other problems. Pyromanic backpackers camping night after night in the same popular spots soon scour the ground of all burnable dead and downed wood—which should, in any case, be left to decay, thereby enriching and renewing the soil. In a mindless quest for their nightly fire fix, many campers turn to breaking dead limbs off standing trees, then to chopping limbs off live trees, scarring what should have been a pristine forest. A fire's intense, concentrated heat sterilizes the soil beneath it and in its immediate vicinity. Even if the rocks of the fire ring are removed and the ashes scattered, the ground will remain lifeless for years, if not decades. Careless fire-builders have also caused numerous forest fires. Too many people have broken camp and left behind a fire that they were sure was out—when it wasn't. Hours or days later, the smoldering embers sprang to life and ignited an inferno. In Shenandoah, Grand Canyon, and Mount Rainier national parks, among others, fires are simply banned in the backcountry. In Yosemite, they're banned above 9,600 feet because all the burnable wood at those rarefied heights has been burned. Below 9,600 feet, they're allowed only in existing fire rings. In Rocky Mountain National Park, fires are permitted at only a dwindling number of backcountry sites. After campers burn everything flammable within a half-mile radius, the site is closed to fires, and the fire ring is removed. In all places where fires are permitted, only dead, downed wood may be burned. One of the lightweight backpacking stoves described earlier provides a far more convenient alternative for cooking than a wood fire: faster to light, easier to regulate, and useful in any weather. And you save yourself the weight of a hatchet, saw, and guilty conscience.

An argument is sometimes made that a fire on a beach that is well supplied with driftwood, constructed below the high-tide mark where all evidence will soon wash away, is acceptable. Or that in really remote country, where very few people go, a small fire can be condoned if all traces are erased. Frankly, I don't buy it. I remember picking over the remnants of a fire on a Grand Canyon beach, striving to locate and pick up every ash for removal. It was impossible. Even after my best efforts, the sand was still peppered with charcoal flakes. What is today remote country, hardly ever visited, is likely to be heavily traveled all too soon. Even if it is not, what right do we have to remake *every* part of the world to our own fancy? Let's make it our goal to leave untouched, forever, that last, tiny, dwindling fragment of the earth that has somehow miraculously escaped human encroachment until now.

LITTER

It should go without saying, but I guess it has to be said, because I still see litter along the trails: *pack out what you pack in*. Then add a double handful or two of other people's trash. On popular trails (popular with litterers, at any rate), I sometimes hike with a small plastic bag in my hands to accommodate the trash I pick up. That keeps my pockets from bulging with stinky cigarette butts and allows me to refrain from imposing on my companions by stuffing trash in one of their outside pack pockets. Burying trash is not acceptable: it will soon be unearthed by rodents, birds, or frost action and scattered in the four directions. Nor will much of it decompose in your lifetime. By one estimate, a steel ("tin") can takes 20 to 40 years to decompose in a wet climate, 100 years to vanish in a dry one. A thin polyethylene bag will mar the landscape for 10 to 20 years; thicker plastics can easily take 50 to 80 years. Aluminum cans will scream "A slob was here!" for 80 to 100 years, perhaps as much as 500. A glass bottle may last 1,000 years—some people say 1,000,000. Food scraps, including things like apple cores and orange peels, should also be packed out. Orange peels take anywhere from one week to six months to decompose beyond recognition. Don't feed the animals, either deliberately or inadvertently. (Actually, there are three exceptions, but I don't imagine you'll want to take me up on this. You can, to your heart's content, feed the mosquitoes, ticks and deerflies.) Feeding creatures that don't normally consume human flesh and blood disrupts their natural eating habits, makes them dependent on human food, and turns them into pests that will eat holes in your pack in search of goodies. Bears that learn to associate people and gear with food can become so aggressive that rangers feel compelled to destroy them. When you get out, recycle what you can—your trash won't decompose any faster in the landfill than it will in the backcountry. Recycling saves energy as well as reducing the need for new landfills. For example, making aluminum cans from recycled aluminum uses 90 percent less energy than making them from scratch. The energy saved from making one aluminum can from recycled aluminum will operate a TV set for three hours.

SANITATION

Until recently, you'd have been thought rather peculiar *not* to leave three things behind in the wilderness: urine, feces and toilet paper. Leaving behind the first is still always acceptable. Urine is relatively innocuous, since it rarely contains significant quantities of bacteria. In well-watered climates, simply get out of sight of the trail and at least 200 feet from any lakes or streams. Heavily used desert regions like the river corridor through the Grand Canyon are a different story. Beaches there are used so intensively by river runners and backpackers that if everyone urinated on the sand, the beach would soon stink of uric acid. The only solution there is to urinate directly into the river, which is flowing by at a rate of tens of thousands of gallons per second.

Leaving behind the second item—feces—is still okay in most areas, but not in all. The goal in disposing of feces is to promote rapid decomposition and to prevent the spread of bacteria from the feces to the water supply or to insects which will then land on your food. First, locate a site at least 200 feet from flowing or standing water or a marshy area. Avoid dry watercourses that may become streams in the rainy season. Try to find a place where you can easily dig a hole 4 to 6 inches deep. Don't dig deeper than that; the organic soil in many alpine areas is only that deep. If you dig deeper, you may go below the zone that supports the active bacteria which hasten decomposition. Avoid pure sand for the same reason. In many regions, digging an adequate hole requires carrying a small trowel. For years I resisted carrying the extra weight, thinking, "Aw, shucks, I can just dig a hole with my boot heel." It doesn't work, at least in a lot of places. Carry a trowel. Do your job thoroughly. My trowel, a sturdy steel-bladed model, weighs less than 6 ounces. When you're done, refill the hole. If you're digging a hole in a grassy region, try to remove the sod in one piece, then replace it carefully. In really remote regions above the timberline, where you're certain no one will stumble across your handiwork for weeks, it may be preferable to deposit waste on the surface rather than digging a hole in the shallow and easily damaged soil. When you're done, spread the feces out with a rock to promote desiccation and decomposition. Properly disposed off, feces should vanish in one to four weeks.

In the winter, in snow country, digging a hole into the ground will be difficult to impossible depending on snow depth and how hard the ground is frozen. The best solution now, given the relatively low numbers of people who go into the backcountry in winter, is to deposit your waste a long ways—like 100 yards—from watercourses, lakes, and any place where a summer hiker is likely to go, literally or figuratively. In Rocky Mountain National Park, backpackers are forbidden to camp within 100 feet of a designated summer site for precisely this reason. If possible, locate a tree well (an area surrounding a tree where the snow pack is shallow) so there's at least a chance of feces getting down to ground level and beginning to decompose quickly come spring. In most areas, so far, this approach is working, given the relatively low level of overnight winter use. If use goes up, or if winter campers are careless about sanitation, this approach may present a problem. On Mount McKinley, for example, traffic on the popular West Buttress route is so heavy in peak season that snow contamination is a real threat to climbers' health, since snow is the only source of water and no one wants to go too far from camp for fear of crevasses. At

17,200 feet, a harsh, windswept basin where climbers congregate in preparation for the summit push, clots of brown turds and toilet paper dot the landscape. Climbers are now required to defecate into a large plastic garbage bag, then throw the bag into the nearest large crevasse. All trash, however, must be carried off the mountain. No trash disposal into crevasses is allowed. If human waste becomes a problem in the mountains of the Lower 48, land managers may start requiring backpackers to pack out everything. River runners in the Grand Canyon have been required to carry out all feces and toilet paper since 1979. As distasteful as this may at first appear, it is absolutely essential, given that the narrow river corridor, with its limited number of campsites, receives over 160,000 user-nights every year, mostly in a five-month period.

In times past, it was considered acceptable to bury toilet paper alongside the feces. Too often, however, people failed to dig a deep enough hole to adequately bury everything. Or perhaps rodents dug into the hole, uncovering the toilet paper and scattering it about. "Toilet-paper flowers" have become one of the most common forms of visible trash. I've seen scraps of toilet paper protruding from the sand smack in the middle of the trail alongside Utah's Paria River and in less obvious but equally unsightly places in Grand Canyon and Canyonlands national parks. Near timberline on Twin Sisters Peak, in Rocky Mountain National Park, I came across an incredibly twisted and ancient limber pine, a stalwart survivor of hundreds of years of winter storms. Entranced, I grabbed my camera and began circling the tree, searching for the most evocative angle. In my preoccupation, I nearly stepped into several piles of feces, complete with toilet paper, that more than one utterly irresponsible hiker had deposited on the ground at the base of this marvelous monument to nature's perseverance. Setting up my tripod with care to keep the tripod legs away from the sewage, I composed a photograph that excluded the mess at my feet— only to discover that some idiotic backpacker had taken a saw to one of the magnificent trees' gnarled limbs. To me, that whole scene represented vandalism far more offensive than the repugnant scrawls found on city bathroom walls.

The solution to these disgusting scenes is simple: pack out your toilet paper. Canyonlands and Grand Canyon national parks already require backpackers to do just that. Rocky Mountain National Park allows backpackers to burn their toilet paper, but the practice leaves much to be desired. If it's raining, the paper won't burn. In any weather, it often doesn't burn completely. Or a gust of wind picks it up when you least expect it and wafts it off to who knows where. An outdoor-education instructor in Canyonlands once set off a minor grass fire trying to burn his toilet paper. He spent several hours busily trying to erase the evidence of his good intentions gone awry. Attempts to burn toilet paper have caused several significant fires in the Grand Canyon, and in 1989 a federal judge in Washington found a hiker liable for $132,700 in fire fighting costs after his attempt to burn his toilet paper ignited a 450-acre forest fire. I carry used toilet paper in a doubled plastic bag that rides inside the clean toilet-paper bag. In some situations, natural substitutes for toilet paper work very well. Smooth rocks and sticks, smooth broad leaves from various plants (watch out for poison ivy!) and snow all work well.

When you're done, if possible, wash your hands using a small amount of biodegradable soap. Don't wash your hands in a lake or stream. Instead, have a companion pour water from a water bottle or pot over your hands while you scrub and rinse 200 feet from any water source.

NOISE AND VISUAL POLLUTION

Two more subtle forms of pollution deserve a mention: noise pollution and visual pollution. We all know that we're rarely the only people out there enjoying the woods on any given day, but why emphasize that fact by making excessive noise? Shouting, banging pots and pans (except when a bear is threatening to steal your M&Ms), or, heaven forbid, bringing a radio or tape player into the woods destroys the illusion of solitude and disturbs wildlife. Noise carries a long way over a mountain lake or in a stone-walled canyon. Keep the racket to a minimum. Large groups should exercise particular care in this regard.

Visual pollution is a tougher issue. Intense, brilliant colors and jarring color combinations are all the rage these days for clothing, packs and, to a lesser extent, tents. Brightly colored gear stands out boldly against the greens, browns, and whites of the summer and winter wilderness. Some people argue that using flashy gear diminishes the feeling of solitude a wilderness should offer because other hikers and their camps stand out like searchlight beacons half a mile away. Others argue that bright clothing and tents could help rescuers trying to locate victims in an emergency or, more selfishly, that vibrant colors make photographs look better. Personally, I find the most garish equipment distasteful and offensive, not so much because it represents visual pollution, as because it seems ostentatious and affected. To learn the lessons that a wilderness sojourn can offer, to preserve the fragile portions of the wilderness and to stay alive in the face of forces vastly greater than ourselves, we need to enter the wilderness in a spirit of humility, almost reverence. Donning some puce, chartreuse, and aquamarine garment seems antithetical to that spirit. With that said, I must admit that I like cheerful colors, and I do not eschew reds and yellows. Movement catches my eye as much as color when I glance across a lake or meadow and spot some other hiker. Designated campsites, at least in Rocky Mountain National Park, are always out of sight of each other. In Shenandoah and Great Smoky Mountains national parks, backpackers are required to camp out of sight of each other, even if they're half a mile apart. Tent color makes no difference if you can't see the neighboring tent. Perhaps the best advice I can offer is to think about the effect of your color choices on your own consciousness as well as your fellow hikers when choosing your gear.

PITCHING CAMP WITHOUT PITCHING A FIT

Enough lecturing on the dos and don'ts. Let's say you've reached the designated site that you reserved, or selected a previously used but environmentally sound site or, if it's the most appropriate, located a completely untouched site that you plan to leave that way. What's the first order of business?

If the afternoon is waning or a thunderstorm is threatening, erecting the tent takes top priority. Most tents have an uncoated canopy with a waterproof fly. If you pitch your tent during a real downpour, the canopy, and hence the tent interior, will get damp if not soaked before you can attach the waterproof fly. Many thunderstorms are brief; if you arrive at camp in the rain, it may be best to wait until the storm passes before setting up the tent. If the storm looks unrelenting, your only recourse is to pitch the tent as fast as you can. Avoid the temptation to bring your soaking wet pack and sopping rain gear into the tent with you. You'll bring in so much moisture that condensation on the tent roof will be almost inevitable. Instead, unload the contents of your pack into the tent as quickly as possible. The contents should be drier than the pack itself if you packed everything in stuff sacks and plastic bags, as you should. Then shed your rain gear, stuff it into your pack, and jump inside. Carrying a sponge will help you mop up whatever moisture does creep inside as well as soak up condensation on the walls or a cup of tea that gets spilled. In rainy country, a tent with a vestibule or rain fly that overhangs the door prevents rain from falling into the tent when the door is open, making it easier to unload gear and keep it and the tent dry.

Select the most level site you can; what seems to be a small tilt when looking down from an erect position will undergo a surprising magnification once you lie down. Even a slight tilt is usually sufficient to promote a caterpillar creep toward the lower end of your sleeping pad as you toss and turn during the night. Lying down is the most certain way to determine an acceptable degree of tilt and to determine which end of the tent is higher. In general, your head should occupy the high ground.

TO PITCH A TENT IN A HIGH
WIND, SPREAD IT OUT FLAT
AND ANCHOR THE CORNERS;
THEN . . .

INSERT THE POLES INTO THE
TENT'S POLE SLEEVES OR
ATTACH THE TENT TO THE
POLES WITH PLASTIC CLIPS;
THEN . . .

ATTACH THE FLY. SOME
TENTS CANNOT BE
ANCHORED BEFORE THE
POLES ARE INSERTED INTO
THEIR SLEEVES.

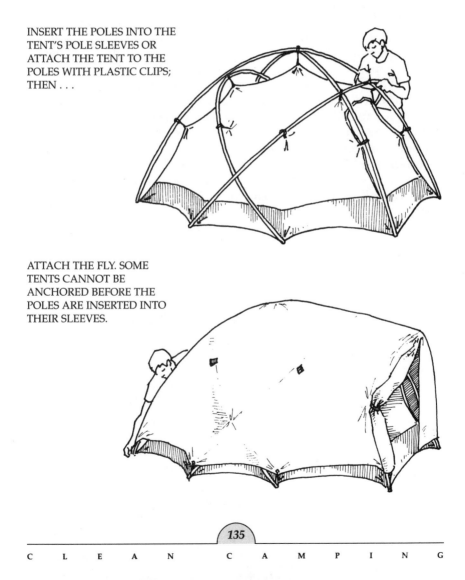

It's important to remove small stones and sticks from your site before erecting the tent to protect both you and the tent floor, but be sure to replace them if you're camping someplace no one has ever camped before. Don't camp in low spots, where puddles will form if it rains. Your tent may have a "waterproof" floor with "sealed" seams, but it isn't a boat. Don't assume it's as seaworthy as Noah's Ark.

So many varieties of tents exist today that it's impossible to give specific advice on pitching each type, but a few general hints may be helpful. Most importantly, be sure to master a new tent's idiosyncrasies by pitching it at home in your front yard or living room a couple of times before heading into the woods. That way you won't be inserting the right pole in the wrong pole sleeve on some pitch-black, frigid night with the rain pelting down.

In high winds, stake out the corners of most tents first, before inserting the poles. With a few tents, staking the corners first can inhibit or prevent inserting the poles. Treat your poles with care. Nicking fiberglass poles or denting aluminum ones will weaken them significantly. When assembling the poles, make sure that each pole segment's end is inserted fully into the neighboring segment's sleeve. The quickest way to break a pole, besides fending off grizzlies with it, is to flex a pole joint when the mating halves have not been fully inserted. The second quickest way is to bend a pole into a tighter curve than it assumes when the tent is pitched. Don't let the ends of the pole segments snap together which can nick the pole ends and abrade the shock cord. Keep the poles clean; don't let grit and dirt enter the pole joints, which can jam shut.

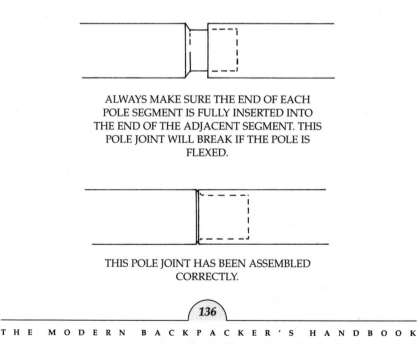

ALWAYS MAKE SURE THE END OF EACH
POLE SEGMENT IS FULLY INSERTED INTO
THE END OF THE ADJACENT SEGMENT. THIS
POLE JOINT WILL BREAK IF THE POLE IS
FLEXED.

THIS POLE JOINT HAS BEEN ASSEMBLED
CORRECTLY.

Many tents today are freestanding, meaning they don't need to be staked to stand upright. They *must* be staked, however, to prevent them from blowing away like expensive high-tech tumbleweeds. I was standing with some hapless rock climbers once at the base of a crag when they happened to glance down into the meadow half a mile away and saw, to their horror, their tent rolling and bouncing across the field, driven by the downdraft from a looming thunderstorm, looking for all the world like the monstrous white ball that always overtook and swallowed the fleeing star of the old TV series, "The Prisoner." The tent continued its lumbering, ungainly journey for fully a quarter-mile across the meadow until finally coming to rest, torn and battered, against the edge of the forest. Moral: always stake your tent! In sand, on very hard ground and on slickrock, where stakes work poorly or not at all, rocks weighing at least 20 pounds apiece form good anchors. If smaller rocks are the only ones available, tie a stout cord coming from the tent around one, then pile rocks on top to anchor the bottom stone. Stuff sacks full of sand or small rocks also make good anchors. To keep grit out of your stuff sacks, turn them inside out before filling them. Don't rely on a couple of sleeping bags tossed inside the tent to weight it down. The tent will take off like a nylon clothes dryer with the sleeping bags tossing about inside.

As a general rule, rocks and logs form better tent anchors in summer than stakes do. Wire stakes—the kind that come with many tents—have little holding power; plastic ones frequently break. Just be sure that if you uproot rocks to anchor your tent, you replace them where you found them when you leave.

COMFORT IN CAMP

For me, the first night or two in a sleeping bag is always a bit restless. Hard ground and the confinement of a sleeping bag are a big change from the luxury of a queen-size bed and flannel sheets. That minor discomfort and many others vanish after a few days, and I quickly begin to feel much more at home in the wilderness. I don't know of any shortcuts to sleeping-bag adaptation—unless you want to bivy in your backyard for a night or two before the trip.

Sleeping cold is a preventable problem even on the first night. The first line of defense, of course, is an adequate sleeping bag and, equally important but sometimes neglected, adequate insulation beneath you in the form of your sleeping pad. Some people have a philosophical objection to sleeping in their clothes. They choose to sleep in the buff under the stares—er, stars. Don't ignore how much warmth those clothes can give. I like to sleep in enough clothes that I can slip out of the bag at night or in the early morning without immediately feeling uncomfortable. In the winter, I often even wear my shell gear.

In addition to wearing adequate clothes, make sure you go to bed warm and well fed. A nightcap of hot chocolate or tea is a great way to start a cozy night's slumber (although unfortunates with small bladders may prefer different methods). If you go to bed cold, it can take a long time to warm up even in the best sleeping bag. Be sure you use your bag to its fullest extent. It's easy to slide into the sack on a cool but not cold evening and fall asleep without cinching down the hood, then awaken at 2:00 A.M. uncomfortably chilled and spend the rest of the night clutching the bag around your shoulders, trying to warm up. Many people in that situation fail to realize how much heat they lose through the mouth of the bag. Take the time to carefully fasten the sleeping bag collar (if it has one) around your neck, then cinch down the hood leaving just your nose, mouth and eyes exposed. Try not to breathe inside the bag. You'll cause condensation that will soak your insulation.

Close confinement inside a tent during a prolonged storm can erode even the closest of friendships. Minor quirks and innocuous habits that are easily overlooked in the city can mushroom into major irritants in the backcountry. David Roberts, in his book about an attempt to climb Alaska's Mount Deborah with Don Jensen, wrote how he "learned to loathe the way Jensen ate his soup." I've felt the same irritation, utterly irrational but real, during long, demanding expeditions in the Alaska Range when my partner chose to snack on an item he had saved after I had already eaten my rations for the day. Ask for your tentmate's okay before you start chomping on another stick of bubble gum. Look into her glowering eyes before humming the twenty-fifth repetition of "Having My Baby." A little extra empathy will defuse most problems before the spark hits the dynamite.

When the sun finally does begin to shine again, the first priority is often to dry out the gear that inevitably became soggy during the storm. Condensation can soak the inside of a tent fly even if no precipitation fell during the night. If you plan to move on that day, remove the tent fly as soon as you get up, and spread it upside down on a rock or branch to dry. You'll save yourself carrying the extra weight of a soaking-wet tent, and you'll help preserve the coatings on the tent fabrics. You can usually pick up a freestanding tent by the poles (after unstaking it) and shake loose dirt out the door before striking it. Be sure to pick up the inevitable twist-tie or candy-wrapper scrap that emerges from hiding when you do so.

Before leaving your site, scour the ground of all bits of trash, big or small, yours or the previous party's. If the site has never been used before (or looks that way), be sure to leave it just the way you found it. Restore natural litter to the tent site and replace any rocks you may have moved. Give others the same pleasure you enjoyed when you chanced upon such a pristine, perfect site.

Some novices worry about thieves stealing gear left behind at a backcountry camp while the owners go for a day hike. Or they worry about being assaulted. Fortunately, such incidents, while not unknown, are very rare. In Rocky Mountain National Park, for example, no backcountry thefts or assaults were reported in 1991, although the park recorded 37,500 backcountry user-nights. Two incidents were reported where mountaineers had bivouac gear vandalized. Other national parks report similar statistics. Backcountry crime is nothing to lose sleep over.

Car break-ins at trail head parking lots are a bigger but still manageable problem. There's not much you can do about car clouting, except to avoid leaving valuables in your car. If you must leave something worth stealing, be sure it's out of sight when you leave. Thieves have been known to hang around and see who leaves what choice items in which trunk. Consider stopping some distance away from your final destination, stashing your valuables out of sight in your trunk, then driving to the trail head and hitting the trail. Not all thieves are human: bears have also been caught clouting cars, although they're usually more interested in the bread in your cooler than the bread in your wallet. Yosemite National Park recommends that hikers avoid storing odorous food anywhere in their cars and avoid storing food or items resembling food anywhere in plain sight. With any luck, your car will be fine when you return.

WILDERNESS KITCHENCRAFT

"Nearness to nature . . . keeps the spirit
sensitive to impressions not commonly felt,
and in touch with the unseen powers."

—Ohiyesa, *The Soul of the Indian*, 1911

y friend Steve Glenn and I were experienced rock climbers but novice backpackers when we ventured unwittingly into one of the most notoriously bear-infested backcountry regions in the nation: Little Yosemite Valley. We did know, however— because the rangers had told us—that we were supposed to hang our food from a tree to keep the bears from getting it. So when we arrived in camp, we picked the nearest tree, tossed a flimsy bit of twine over a spindly branch about 8 feet off the ground, tied our food bag to the end of the twine, and hauled it up as far as it could go.

It was almost dark when we glimpsed a large, furry and very intimidating shape moving toward us through the trees, followed by two smaller shapes. A mother black bear and her two cubs were starting their nightly rounds. Soon the entire family was prowling the outskirts of our camp. We realized immediately that we had hung our precious provisions at precisely the right height for a bear punching bag. I began having nightmares of ascending Half Dome the next day as my empty stomach and calorie-starved muscles traded insults. In a last, desperate attempt to save our food, we mobilized our only weapon— our vocal cords—punctuating our shouts with the cacophony of pots and pans smashed together. The bears yawned. They'd heard all this before. Sure of their ultimate victory, they retreated briefly, and we seized the opportunity to grab our food and hustle over to the "bear-proof" food-hanging cable the rangers had installed. One end of the cable was anchored to a tree about 20 feet off the ground. The cable then ran horizontally to a pulley at the same height on an adjacent tree, then down through the pulley to a stout spring-loaded clip attached to an eyebolt firmly embedded in the tree's base. The cable continued below the eyebolt, providing the slack necessary to lower the cable and attach the food. We unhooked the clip, lowered the cable, tied our food to the middle of the cable between the two trees and hoisted it back up, leaving the food 20 feet off the ground exactly in the middle between the two trees. With the bears advancing upon us once more, we retreated, smugly satisfied that we would indeed have something edible to fuel our climb the next day.

The mother bear, who had watched all this commotion from a slight distance, now strolled up and deftly climbed the tree supporting the pulley end of the cable. The food bag was hanging at least 10 feet out from the tree trunk, far beyond her reach as she clung to the tree, and we were certain she wouldn't even come close to stealing our food. We soon learned that we had underestimated her intelligence. Once at the height of the cable, she reached out and gave the cable a mighty downward jerk, setting our food bag to swinging toward her like a pendulum. As the bag neared the apex of its arc, the bear took a swing at it with a massive paw. Even a glancing contact would have shredded the bag and dropped its contents to the hungry cubs waiting below, but she missed by inches. By sheer luck, we had tied the bag to the cable with a short enough string to keep the bag from swinging within the bear's reach.

When her repeated jerk-and-slash technique proved futile, she descended the tree, grabbed the free end of the cable in her teeth, and began yanking, evidently hoping to break the eyebolt or the clip anchoring the lower end of the cable. Still she was defeated, and our hopes rose that she would soon abandon her efforts. Then she turned her attention to the clip itself. Less than a minute later, she found a way to unlatch it, and our food plummeted to the ground. The cubs pounced on the defenseless bag, and all our hopes of breakfast vanished into their hungry gullets. Steve and I climbed Half Dome the next day with the hypoglycemic blues, then ran back down to the floor of Yosemite Valley, where I came as close as I've ever come to literally eating myself sick.

PROTECTING YOUR FOOD

Before you hurl this book into a bonfire and vow never to set foot off pavement again, let me hasten to add that this was not only the

first, but also the last time I have ever lost food to bears in nearly twenty years of backpacking. I've never even seen a bear in Rocky Mountain National Park, where I've done much of my backpacking, much less had to battle one for my breakfast. Except in a few places where black bears have learned that backpackers mean packs full of food, your chances of seeing a bear are actually slight. According to information from Shenandoah National Park, only one visitor in 1 million to North American parks is injured by a bear. You might say it's a bearly perceptible risk. Even in places like Little Yosemite Valley, you can protect your food from black bears if you know what to do.

All Yosemite bears, and most bears in other parts of the Lower 48, are black bears, which are persistent and intelligent, but basically timid. Yellowstone and Glacier national parks and many parks in Alaska are also home to grizzly bears, which are far more aggressive and dangerous than black bears. The food-hanging method described below will work fairly well with either kind of bear. Personally defending your food from an oncoming bear—a risky proposition at best—can sometimes work with more timid black bears (see page 143 for more details on this) but is never recommended with grizzlies.

The most bear-resistant method of storing food is called the counterweight method. All provisions should be stored with this method at all times except when you're actually preparing a meal. Never store food in your tent or pack. That's a sure way to lose both your food and your equipment. Make sure you stash odoriferous non-food items in your food bag as well. Potential bear attractants include garbage, toothpaste, sunscreen, and perfume. Now find a suitable tree. You're looking for one with a live branch 17 or more feet off the ground that's still 1 inch in diameter 10 feet from the trunk. Basically, the idea is to find a branch that's strong enough to support your food's weight, but not so strong that a cub could crawl out it and swipe your food. The tree must lack strong branches beneath the food-hanging branch that could serve as a platform for a bear. Although such trees may seem as common as unicorns, persist and you will be rewarded. Tie a rock to the end of a stout cord 40 or 50 feet long and toss the rock over the branch. Separate your food into two bags of roughly equal weight and tie the first bag to the cord. Hang your cooking pots with the food so you'll have a warning if a bear does come marauding. Haul the first bag up to the branch and tie the second bag to the cord as high as you can reach. Leave a loop of cord hanging out, and put the remainder of the cord inside the bag. Push the second bag up with a long stick until the two bags hang side by side. To retrieve the food, snag the loop with the stick and pull the bag down gently.

This Fort Knox method should suffice to defend your food against most bears. It should also protect it against chipmunks and

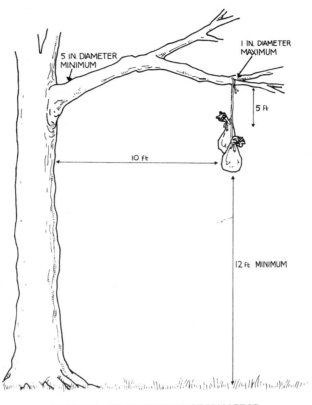

THE FORT KNOX METHOD OF HANGING
FOOD IN BEAR COUNTRY.

squirrels, which are a much more common threat. I've returned to my pack after leaving it alone for just five minutes and discovered a human-habituated marmot stealing my peanut-butter-and-jelly sandwich from an open pack pocket. To add insult to injury, a pair of hikers was standing nearby enjoying the fat rascal's bold performance and doing nothing to intervene. On several occasions, I've had witless rodents chew their way into a pack pocket even though there was no food inside. To discourage such damage, leave your pack open and empty with the pockets unzipped when you go to bed.

Yosemite rangers advise backpackers that even the best method of hanging food is simply a delaying tactic when the prowler is a black bear accustomed to stealing from humans. Rangers urge backpackers who are confronted with a black bear to make noise, throw rocks, and chase the bear vigorously. The more people who chase the bear, and the longer and farther they chase it, the better. Don't get carried away, however. You should never corner a bear, nor come between a mother bear and her cubs. If a bear does manage to steal some of your food, leave the bear alone until he abandons it. Bears are like two-year-olds: they haven't learned to clean up after themselves, so you'll have to do it for them. Pack out everything the bear doesn't eat. Don't leave it as litter to entice other bears or ruin the next visitor's enjoyment of the wilderness.

If you are backpacking in grizzly country, you must take additional precautions. In Denali National Park, where suitable food-hanging trees scarcely exist, backpackers are required to carry their food in bearproof containers issued by the park. Rangers further recommend that backpackers refrain from cooking in even a well-ventilated tent. The cooking odors can permeate the nylon and attract bears even if you stash your food elsewhere. While cooking, be prepared to store your food quickly in its bearproof container. Keep your other gear packed so you can leave immediately, leaving nothing behind, if a bear suddenly intrudes. The goal is to prevent an aggressive grizzly from receiving a reward for its intrusion. After cooking dinner, move on a mile or two before making camp.

To avoid startling a grizzly who may be invisible in deep brush, make noise as you walk. Some people tie a bell to their pack or rattle pebbles in a can. Others sing, talk or chant high-school fight songs. Pay attention to your surroundings so you know when bears are nearby. A bear's five-toed paw print is as long as a human's but twice as wide. The claw marks extend well beyond the paw print itself. A bear's droppings are massive, often resembling a cow's. After the berries ripen, droppings may consist of a pile of partially digested berries.

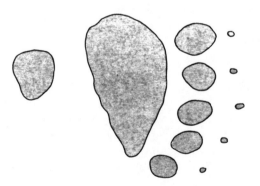

A GRIZZLY PAW PRINT, ABOUT TWO-THIRDS
LIFE-SIZE.

If you encounter a grizzly, refrain from approaching it. Grizzlies can start to feel threatened even if you're 100 yards away. Bears will defend their cubs, their territory, their food and themselves. If you spot a feeding grizzly that is unaware of your presence, retreat slowly when the bear's attention is absorbed by its food. If the bear becomes aware of you and approaches, remain calm—or, if that's impossible, at least try to *look* calm. Hold up your arms, speak firmly and confidently to the bear, and back away slowly. The idea is to let the bear know that you're not a threat. Don't turn and run—you can't outrun a grizzly. If there is a suitable tree nearby, climb it, but remember that a grizzly standing on its hind legs can reach 10 feet. If the grizzly stands up and waves its nose in the air, it's trying to identify you. Talking to the bear and waving your arms helps it do so. If the bear makes a series of woofs and grunts, it's challenging you to either fight or leave. If it stands sideways, it's displaying its size in an attempt to intimidate you. Take the hint: retreat slowly. If the bear charges you, stand your ground. In most cases, charges are bluffs. If the bear calls *your* bluff and is about to strike, fall to the ground, keeping your pack on, and play dead. Do not abandon your pack, except as a last resort. Don't inadvertently teach the grizzly that charging hikers is an easy way to get a meal.

In a very real sense, grizzly country belongs to the bears. They are the dominant predators, not humans. Tread with caution.

On Mount McKinley, ravens wreak havoc with unprotected food caches as high as 16,000 feet. I have never seen ravens attack a hanging food bag in the Lower 48, but one incident in the Escalante region of Utah raised my suspicions. Cora and I had hung our food from a tree and were leaving camp for a day-hike when two ravens flew into our campsite. I knew from my experience on McKinley that a raven's powerful beak could shred our tough nylon food sacks in seconds. With two days to go on our trip, and no desire to seek visions through a 48-hour fast, I retrieved the food bag and carried it with us throughout the day-hike. Paranoid? Perhaps. Hungry? No way.

STOVE SAFETY

A friend once lost half his tent—and half his hair—when his stove overheated and the pressure-relief valve burst open and spewed a two-foot arc of flame. Two experienced Swiss mountaineers died on Mount McKinley in 1986 from carbon-monoxide poisoning caused by operating a stove in an unventilated tent. If mishandled, every type of stove and every kind of stove fuel can cause an accident that destroys expensive equipment and inflicts severe burns. All stoves produce carbon monoxide, a deadly, *odorless* gas. To operate a stove safely, you must know and follow these simple rules.

Never fill a liquid-fueled stove or change the cartridge on a butane-powered stove near a source of heat or sparks. If you are using a liquid-fueled stove, be sure to use a funnel when filling it to reduce the chance of a spill that could accidentally ignite. Never refill a liquid-fueled stove while it's hot. To avoid temptation when you're hungry and impatient for dinner, make sure the stove is full before you start cooking. That way you won't run out of fuel in the middle of preparing your salmon soufflé. Most stoves should be filled only three-quarters full to allow room for an air space. Pumps actually compress air, not fuel. The compressed air then drives the fuel out of the tank and up to the burner.

All reputable backpacking stoves come with explicit lighting directions, but a few general pointers may be helpful. First, never lean over any stove while lighting it: it could flare up and singe your eyebrows, or worse. Never light or operate a stove inside a tent. You risk both burning down your wilderness house and asphyxiating yourself with carbon monoxide. Use the minimum amount of priming fuel possible. Excessive priming is a leading cause of accidents. Make sure that your fuel tank doesn't become overheated, as it might, for example, if you confine it too tightly within some kind of homemade wind-screen system. Liquid-fueled stove tanks will normally be warm but not hot when the stove is running; the cartridge on a butane stove should be cool to the touch. Be sure to carry your liquid-fueled stove and extra fuel separate from your food and pots. Gasoline fumes can permeate food with surprising ease. Finally, if your stove is liquid-fueled, you should expect it to malfunction periodically. Carry a repair kit containing all the little washers and gaskets that are likely to crack or begin to leak. Most backpacking shops carry repair kits for specific brands of stoves. I have never seen a butane stove break down, but I'm sure it has happened. Most of those stoves cannot be readily repaired in the field, so your only option in situations where a stove breakdown would be very serious is to carry a backup stove. I have carried a backup on lengthy Alaskan expeditions, but never while backpacking in the Lower 48.

The amount of fuel you need depends on the efficiency of your stove, the kind of food you're cooking, the wind speed, the altitude and the temperature. Rather than trying to plug all those variables into some formula, try this approach. Most stove instruction manuals give running time on a tankful of fuel. Add up the amount of cooking time you anticipate, taking into account the fact that food easily takes 20 percent longer to cook above 10,000 feet than it does at sea level, then give yourself a 25 percent safety margin. Don't forget to add in the time it takes water to come to a boil as well as the actual cooking time. You'll probably come home with a lot of extra fuel, but that's better than the alternative. Stretching food is easy. Stretching fuel is not, and many backpacking foods are completely indigestible unless they're cooked. In the summer, Cora and I find that we go through one 6.75-ounce butane cartridge in about three days with our Bleuet 206, running our stove about 45 to 60 minutes per day. A two-person team using a liquid-fueled stove might go through 2 or 3 ounces of fuel each day. Fuel consumption with either kind of stove will be much higher if you have to melt snow for water. On McKinley, a two-person team using a white-gas stove will burn a minimum of 8 ounces of fuel per day. Two-person teams using 6.75-ounce butane cartridges usually figure on one cartridge lasting a day and a half. These figures assume the use of freeze-dried food that doesn't require cooking. You'll need more if you're boiling noninstant rice or macaroni. Bring plenty of fuel on your first few trips with a new stove and log the amount you actually burn. You'll soon know how much you need.

KITCHEN CHORES

You may go backpacking to "get away from it all," but there's one thing you never really get away from: washing dishes. As a first step toward simplifying the process, try to cook only as much as you can eat, so you don't have any leftovers. If some food does remain, put it in your garbage bag and pack it out. You may need to double-bag the leftovers to prevent the garbage bag from leaking inside your pack. Burying leftovers will only encourage rodents, camp-robbing blue jays, and bears to come calling.

Cora and I have tried bringing various scrubbing pads to clean our pot, but found that they clung to food particles, which rotted quickly and stank. If you're in sandy or snowy country, scrape the pot as clean as possible with a spoon, then scrub it with a handful of sand or a snowball. If your local soils turn uncooperatively to mud, persist with the spoon, aided by the application of warm water. On short trips, we carry a few squares of paper towel, which we use sparingly to polish off the last spots of grease. We also sterilize the pot every day by boiling clean water in it. You can use the hot water to make a cup of tea or as the first step in boiling pasta or rice. While the water is boiling, dip your utensils in to sterilize them as well. Dishwashing soap is generally unnecessary in the backcountry. Even biodegradable soap pollutes streams, and it's hard to rinse away soap completely. Any residue that remains becomes an unpleasantly effective laxative. Refrain from washing or rinsing pots or dishes in any stream or lake. Instead, carry your dishwater and rinse water at least 100 feet away from streams or lakes and scatter it on the ground. By the time the water filters back to its source, it will be clean again.

13

TAKING CARE OF SOME BODY—YOURS

"It is life near the bone where it is sweetest."

—Henry Thoreau, *Walden*, 1854

ead this chapter like a newspaper. Sure, there are many things that can go wrong on a backpacking trip. If you dwell on those possibilities the way a newspaper dwells on wars, disasters, and atrocities, you'll probably never want to go hiking again. You need to remember, however, that newspapers never print headlines that read; "The vast majority of the world's people had an OK day today." In the same way, nearly all backpacking trips go off without a hitch. The following discussion of potential backcountry problems will start with the commonplace but annoying and lead up to the life-threatening but exceedingly rare. In the space available, I can provide only a brief overview of what backpackers should know about wilderness medicine. Books dealing with the subject are listed in the Bibliography.

MOSQUITOES

Unfortunately for backpackers, mosquitoes agree with Thoreau that life is sweetest when it's closest to the bone. These voracious pests have probably ruined more trips for poorly prepared backpackers than all the thunderstorms and rainy days put together. When you add in the threat of chiggers, ticks, deerflies and blackflies, it's no wonder that Americans buy some $50 million worth of insect repellent every year.

Nearly all commercial repellents contain DEET, so named because it sounds like the maddening hum of a mosquito about to pounce on your ear just when your hands are fully occupied with draining boiling water off your wilderness pasta. (Actually, it's a contraction for N,N-diethyl-meta-toluamide, which sounds so hideously toxic that you should probably forget you ever knew the real explanation.) Mosquitoes are attracted by the carbon dioxide that people give off. Repellents generally work by masking that odor. When used as directed—the standard caveat—DEET doesn't give most people any problems. A few people suffer minor skin irritations, and my friends tell me that if you get the stuff too close to your lips, it will make them tingle. To reduce the possibility of any problems, use repellent sparingly, keep it away from your face, don't put clothing over repellent-coated skin and wash the repellent off once you come inside. If you do experience problems and want to continue using a repellent, try a product with a lower concentration of DEET or one with a time-release formulation. The incidence of allergic reactions goes up with the concentration.

Even under the best of circumstances, repellents provide only partial protection. A much better solution is to wear pants and a loose-fitting, long-sleeved shirt made of a tightly woven material through which mosquitoes cannot bite. If you find it hard to locate a shirt that's woven sufficiently tightly, add a T-shirt underneath. Mosquitoes find it tough to bite through two layers. Cap off your pants and shirt with a brimmed hat with a skirt that drapes down past your collar, and you'll have put a solid physical barrier between those rapacious mosquitoes and your precious hide. A couple of companies make baseball-style hats with removable skirts. If you don't want to buy something new, attach an old handkerchief to a hat you already have with a few safety pins. You'll look more dashing than a member of the French Foreign Legion, and you'll be contributing personally to a reduction in the mosquito population since female mosquitoes need a meal of mammalian blood to reproduce. Under really grim conditions, substitute a mosquito headnet for the skirted hat. A mosquito headnet is just a bag made of mosquito netting which you pull over a hat with a broad brim. The bag comes down to your collar. Ignore all snide jokes about veiled women and enjoy the insect-free peace. You may also want to wear a pair of light gloves to keep mosquitoes off your hands.

You might object that all this extra clothing must lead to a nuclear meltdown when you're pumping out the miles with a full pack. In practice, however, mosquitoes are rarely a problem when you're walking steadily. It seems to take them a minute or two to find you as you pass through their vicinity. By that time, you've moved out of their territory. I normally wear shorts if I know I'll be walking without interruption. If you sit down for lunch or start to make camp, however, mosquitoes will soon come swarming like ants to spilt honey. Once you've stopped moving, however, extra clothing is much more tolerable.

Mosquitoes operate within a limited range of temperatures. In the high mountains, they usually go to bed at sunset. In the warm lowlands, they may be scarce during the day and active all night. Knowing the local mosquitoes' habits can help you avoid them. All mosquitoes like wet, marshy areas and dislike wind. If you have the choice, make your lunch stops on the ridge crests and passes, and place your camp on a dry, breezy knoll well away from lush meadows.

STOPPING SUNBURN AND BLISTERS

Pants, long-sleeved shirts and skirted hats also provide protection against another backcountry assailant: the sun. Sun-blocking lotions also work well if applied liberally and regularly. Many flatlanders underestimate the intensity of sunlight at high altitudes, particularly if snowfields are adding their reflection to the glare. When I was embarking on an expedition to McKinley in 1982, my assistant, who was quite pale after the long, dark, Alaskan winter, told me that she hoped to come back with a gorgeous tan. I told her, "If you do the absolute best you can to protect yourself, you'll come back with a tan. If you do *any less,* you'll come back peeling like weathered paint."

On McKinley, I put sunscreen on every hour or two; in the Rockies, if I'm not on snow, I put it on twice a day. I like the sunscreens with a SPF (Sun Protection Factor) of 25 or greater, since skin cancer runs in my family. However, even people who tan easily should protect their skin carefully. Also, when applying sunscreen don't forget those easily overlooked places like the backs of your knees and the tops of your ears.

Blisters rank with mosquitoes and sunburn as the miseries that beset backpackers most often. The first defense, of course, is properly fitting boots. The second is to avoid boots that are stiffer than you really need. For ten years now, the trend in outdoor footwear has been toward lighter, more supple boots which are frequently made of a combination of thin leather and Cordura nylon. Many hiking boots these days are soft and pliable when they come off the shelf. If you feel that you simply must own stiff boots, be sure to break them in thoroughly by wearing them around town, then on progressively longer day hikes. This is one area where hidebound traditionalists pay a heavy price.

If a hot spot does start to develop, stop and deal with it immediately, before it erupts into a full-fledged blister. Sometimes the problem can be fixed simply by straightening out a wrinkled sock. On long, steady downhills, it can help to lace your boots extra tight to prevent your feet from sliding forward at each step, thereby blistering the soles and toes. Wearing a thin pair of socks under a thicker pair can also help. If these tactics fail, I employ moleskin, an adhesive-backed feltlike material found in nearly all drugstores. I usually slap a piece of moleskin directly over the hot spot and leave it there for the duration of the trip. If a pair of boots frequently gives me trouble in the same spot, I'll counterpunch by applying moleskin before starting the hike. Don't forget to bring a knife—preferably one with scissors—to cut the sheets of moleskin to the right size; you can't tear it easily, as you can adhesive tape.

If a blister does develop, cover it with something that won't stick to the blister itself, like an adhesive bandage or a piece of moleskin reversed so that the sticky side faces away from your skin. Another possibility is Second Skin, a gellike material that comes in sheets. Second Skin soothes blisters wonderfully. Once you have protected the blister, cover the area with moleskin or tape to keep the protective layer in place.

I'm fortunate that simple preventive measures usually stop me from blistering even when I'm wearing rigid plastic ski-mountaineering boots. Cora, on the other hand, has tried every possible permutation of tape, Band-Aids, moleskin, Second Skin, petroleum jelly, silk socks, and prayer, and still has not found a way to make stiff boots tolerable. The only solution for her is to buy hiking boots that are flexible enough when new that they require no breaking in. Winter is a more difficult problem, since ski boots must be fairly stiff to control your skis. The best solution she has found so far is to apply Second Skin followed by adhesive tape before she starts the ski tour. Fortunately for the rest of us, few people have blister problems as severe as Cora's.

PURIFYING WATER

When I started backpacking, most people drank directly from streams and lakes in alpine regions without bothering to purify the water. After all, mountain streams were literally as pure as the driven snow, right? That was before the word *giardia* began appearing in backpackers' vocabularies and an occasional backpacker's gullet. *Giardia lamblia* is a protozoan parasite which can cause a disease called giardiasis that is characterized by explosive diarrhea, cramps, bloating and vomiting. Carriers of the disease excrete the parasite in the form of

FINDING WATER IN THE DESERT

In the desert, water is life, and your pack is likely to be quite heavy with it. Water weighs 8 pounds per gallon. Since you'll need at least a gallon a day in the warm months—more at the height of summer—planning a backpacking trip in the desert revolves around the quantity of water that you can reasonably carry and the likelihood of finding additional sources along your route. Always carry enough water that if the spring or intermittent stream at your proposed campsite is dry, you can make it back out. Don't count on water being available just because the map shows a spring. You can probably trust people who have actually been there—so long as they were there yesterday, not the week or month before. Even in that case, bring along some extra water.

In an emergency, your map, your eyes, and your trowel are your best bets for finding water. Examine the map not only for springs and streams, but also for man-made structures like wells, cattle tanks, and windmills. As you hike, look for bright

cysts, which can survive for months in water as cold as 32°. Some thirty species of animals, including humans, have been identified as carriers. Treatment is with drugs that produce their own unpleasant side effects; fortunately, many people seem to recover spontaneously without medical intervention. Some hikers tend to downplay the threat, citing statistics showing that less than half of the people who drink water heavily contaminated with giardia cysts actually become infected, and that less than a quarter of those develop symptoms.

The problem with such a Pollyanna-like attitude, of course, is that it's impossible to assess the risk based on a visual inspection of the water. Why take a chance, when avoiding the risk is so easy?

Boiling your drinking water will kill giardia and every other waterborne pathogen that might be lurking in the murk. The time recommended varies widely. Yosemite rangers say three to five minutes, which about splits the difference between the high and low estimates. The disadvantage of boiling is that it consumes a great deal of time, fuel, and patience. More convenient methods are available.

Cora and I use tablets containing a compound, tetraglycine

green vegetation. There may be a seep or spring nearby. Keep an eye out for cottonwoods, sycamores, and seep willows growing in dry streambeds. They, too, may mean water is close at hand. If you find damp sand, dig down with your trowel. You may find water farther down, or you may be able to wait until the depression fills up. Search out places in canyons where flash-flood waters have scoured away the sand and gravel, exposing bedrock. Shallow depressions in the bedrock, called tinajas, may have trapped pools of rainwater. If you're hiking the ridges in hilly terrain, examine the canyon floors below you for the bright flash of sunlight reflecting in a water-filled pothole. Lava and limestone are porous rocks that often contain springs. A cave in a limestone cliff or a place where lava abuts a sandstone cliff may contain a seep or a spring. Look for the dark stains and green moss that mark seeps in sandstone cliffs. In the high desert in the winter months, examine the shady north sides of cliffs, where the sun never shines. Lingering snow patches may provide a source of water. Whatever the source, an easily cleaned water filter will not only remove whatever critters may exist, but also the inevitable sand and silt.

hydroperiodide, which releases iodine when dissolved in water. These tablets are widely available under the name Potable Aqua. Using the tablets is simple: dissolve one tablet in a liter of water and let it sit for ten minutes. If the water is very cold (which most mountain water is) let it sit for twenty minutes. If the water is very cloudy, use two tablets and wait for twenty minutes. Using iodine to purify drinking water will not harm you so long as its use is confined to a few back-packing trips every year. It should not be used for more than a few days at a time.

Iodine tablets gives water a distinct iodine taste, which Cora and I choose to mask by adding a little Nutrasweet Kool-Aid. Nutrasweet Kool-Aid? I hear you cry. Contrary to what you might expect, the lemonade flavor is quite palatable and not overpoweringly sweet when mixed at half-strength. Unlike the Kool-Aid sweetened with sugar, Nutrasweet Kool-Aid weighs next to nothing.

Don't like the notion of gunking up that "pure" wilderness wa-ter with Kool-Aid and can't stand the taste of iodine? Try one of the several brands of water filters now made specifically for backpacking.

Most of these use a microporous filter with a pore size below 1 micron to screen out bacteria and larger organisms such as *Giardia*. In addition, some contain an activated charcoal component which removes many organic compounds such as pesticides. Microporous filters do not claim to strain out viruses, which are far smaller than bacteria. However, at least one hybrid filter currently exists that contains both a microporous filter and a mass of iodinated resin beads. As the water flows past the beads, enough iodine is released to kill viruses so long as the concentration of viruses is moderate. The filtered water has a slight iodine taste, but it's not as noticeable as when using iodine tablets.

Manufacturers of filters that work solely on a microporous principle, without the chemical disinfection necessary to kill viruses, assert that viruses simply aren't an issue in wilderness areas in North America. They're probably right, at least most of the time. You should be concerned about viruses, however, if you're in an undeveloped country and the water you're eyeing suspiciously may be contaminated with sewage from people living upstream. Best solution there: either boil the water vigorously, or use two iodine tablets and wait twenty minutes. If you object to the strong iodine taste, you can then run the water through a filter with an activated charcoal component to remove it.

Backpacking water filters are about the size of a can of motor oil and weigh anywhere from 8 to 24 ounces, while a bottle of Potable Aqua is about the size of your thumb and weighs just 1 ounce. The savings in weight and bulk is another reason why Cora and I prefer using Potable Aqua to carrying a filter. My pack is heavy enough already and besides, I actually *like* Kool-Aid. Don't tell anybody.

HYPOTHERMIA

I regard it as a point of professional pride that I never get cold in the mountains, even in the dead of winter. Of course, that's not to say my pride has never been wounded, sometimes quite uncomfortably so. Nonetheless, I've never actually been hypothermic, the condition in which the body's core temperature drops low enough to impair normal muscular and mental function. If you carry the clothing described earlier in Chapter 2 and use it wisely, you'll never get in serious trouble from hypothermia. Your companion may not be as well prepared or as conscientious about body maintenance as you, however, so you should know the symptoms of hypothermia.

Hypothermia begins with a sensation of chilliness, numb skin, shivering, and loss of coordination and strength in the hands. It progresses to more severe shivering and loss of overall muscular coordination. Victims begin to stumble and fall frequently. Hands become numb, useless claws. Thought and speech slow to a crawl. Severely hypothermic victims lose the ability to walk and become incoherent and irrational. If cooling continues, death occurs because of heart failure.

Treatment for moderately hypothermic victims is simple: rewarming, starting with the trunk. Simply adding more clothing does not help because hypothermia victims have lost the ability to rewarm themselves. Adding more clothing only serves to reduce the rate of heat loss; it does nothing to actually rewarm the body. To do that, external heat must be applied. The easiest way to do that in the field is to zip two sleeping bags together and have a warm rescuer climb inside with the victim. A conscious victim should drink warm liquids; however, you should never try to force unconscious victims to drink. They are likely to choke. Severely hypothermic victims require hospital care.

The key to preventing hypothermia is staying dry. Good shell clothing will ward off rain and snow. Preventing sweat from soaking your clothing is more difficult. If you let yourself sweat while working hard in the cold, you'll get chilled when you stop. Despite the obvious threat of discomfort, however, sweating seems almost impossible to avoid. Why?

Perhaps because, in some primeval way, we like it. Researchers at Kansas State University's Institute for Environmental Research found that people exercising in a test chamber considered themselves more comfortable when they were sweating than when they weren't. The harder they worked, the more sweat they were producing when they declared themselves most comfortable, even though they had the option of cooling the test chamber until they stopped sweating completely.

We also sweat in the cold because the evaporation of sweat inside clothing rarely provides more than half the cooling of sweat evaporating off bare skin. The reason? Some sweat vapor inside a jacket condenses and gives up its heat before it can escape to the outside air. If you are sweating but not cooling, your body responds by producing more sweat in an accelerating cycle that can only be stopped by removing insulation.

In cold weather, you must consciously fight your natural tendency to sweat. That means dressing in layers that can be removed to prevent sweating when you are working hard and added to hold in heat when you stop moving. The human body generates about five times as much heat when hiking with a load as it does when at rest. Savvy backpackers adjust clothing as often as needed to remain comfortable. Since some sweating is almost inevitable, bring dry underlayers to change into when you reach camp.

Hypothermia cases are by no means limited to the winter months. In fact, hypothermia is actually quite common in the *summer*, when inexperienced and poorly prepared hikers get caught above timberline by a 40° rainstorm and 20-mph wind—a potentially lethal combination.

HEAT EXHAUSTION AND HEAT STROKE

Backpackers who venture into the desert in summer face a different set of problems. Heat exhaustion is an easy-to-remedy malady in which the victim feels faint, dizzy, and nauseated. Significantly, however, the victim's core temperature is not elevated above the normal 98.6° F. The solution is to rest in the coolest area available and to drink salty fluids. Most victims recover quickly.

Heatstroke is a far more serious malady in which sweating stops, the skin feels hot to the touch, and the body's core temperature soars to 105° or higher. Heatstroke is a true medical emergency that requires rapid cooling of the victim. If possible, immerse the victim in tepid (not cold) water. If that's not possible, cover the victim with water-soaked clothes and fan the victim to promote evaporation. Massage the victim's limbs vigorously to prevent blood from pooling in the extremities. By increasing circulation, you'll also help cool the overheated core. A heatstroke victim's temperature can be quite unstable for several days afterwards.

The key to preventing heat injuries is to drink. And drink. And drink—up to eight quarts of water per day in extreme conditions. Don't try to conserve water, thinking that you'll "teach your body to make do with less." Your body doesn't work that way. Don't rely on your sensation of thirst to tell you when to drink. You're likely to drink a pint when you need a half-gallon. Your urine should be copious and clear. Dark yellow urine is a sign that you're not drinking enough. Pound those fluids! Wear light-colored clothing and a well-ventilated sun hat with a broad brim or skirt that hangs down over your neck. Schedule your hiking for the early morning and late evening, when temperatures are lower. Find some shade and hole up in the middle of the day. Only mad dogs and overeager backpackers go out in the midday sun when the temperature is in the triple digits.

ALTITUDE ILLNESS

Cora and I often find that we sleep restlessly on the first night of a mountain backpacking trip. The lack of a familiar bed undoubtedly plays a role, but equally important is the sudden change in altitude. Many campsites in the Colorado Rockies are at 10,000 or 11,000 feet. Cora and I live in Boulder, at an elevation of about 5,000 feet. We usually drive to the trail head and hike in on the first day. The abrupt change in altitude is sometimes sufficient to produce a mild version of the malady known as mountain sickness, which is characterized by fitful sleep, loss of appetite, and a persistent headache, particularly at night while lying down. Flatlanders coming up from sea level often experience the same symptoms with greater intensity. For Cora and me, the second night is usually much better than the first, while the third is better still. Drinking plenty of fluids—enough to keep your urine clear—helps prevent mountain sickness. If you can, spend a night at an intermediate elevation, perhaps in a nearby mountain town, before beginning the hike. Most people can adjust well if they give themselves enough time. If you do start to develop uncomfortable symptoms, avoid overexertion, but don't confine yourself to bed. You'll often find that mild exercise actually makes you feel better. If the symptoms persist, descend. Losing several thousand feet of elevation is an almost-certain cure. Backpackers in the Himalayas and Andes, who may be camping at much higher elevations than backpackers in the continental United States, should pick up a manual on mountain sickness and its dangerous cousins, pulmonary and cerebral edema. One good one is Dr. Peter Hackett's book *Acute Mountain Sickness: Prevention, Recognition and Treatment*, published by the American Alpine Club.

POISONOUS SNAKES

We have now gotten so far down on the list of possible wilderness hazards that those remaining are unlikely to affect most hikers during their entire career. Take snakebite, for example. Only about 20 percent of the snake species found in the United States are poisonous. Depending on whom you want to believe, anywhere from 1,000 to 45,000 people are bitten by snakes in the United States every year. Perhaps one-fifth of those bites are from poisonous snakes; however, in about 20 percent of all rattlesnake bites and 30 percent of all cottonmouth and copperhead bites, the snake injects no venom. Estimates of the number of fatal snakebites per year in the United States range from less than a dozen to about 30. Lightning is a bigger cause for worry, as are allergic reactions to bee stings.

Most snakes are afraid of humans and will slither away given half a chance. To avoid surprising one, watch where you walk. Snakes like rocky slopes that catch the morning sun, river bottoms, and any kind of cover: rock piles, brush piles, fallen logs. They congregate in their kitchen: any place where rodents, frogs and lizards abound. Look first before stepping over a log. If you are scrambling in likely snake habitat, don't reach up blindly for a hold you can't see. Most of the high alpine areas in the United States are completely free of snakes, as is Alaska.

If you do get bitten, avoid panic. Every year, people die of fright and unnecessary treatment after being bitten by a nonpoisonous snake.

Even if the snake is poisonous, the chance of its bite killing a healthy adult is small. Toddlers and elderly people are at greater risk. Keep the victim quiet to help retard the spread of the venom and send someone out to get help in evacuating the victim. Clean and bandage the wound. *Do not* apply ice to the bite or attach a tourniquet above the bite. The result can be a disastrous case of gangrene. Do not try to cut open the area surrounding the puncture marks and suck out the venom by mouth. The risk of serious infection is very high, and your incisions can easily damage nerves, tendons and ligaments, particularly if the snake bit a hand or foot. Some authorities recommend snakebite kits, which contain a razor blade to make incisions and some kind of suction device for extracting venom. While these are better than the cut-and-suck-by-mouth method, the danger of infection and cutting vital structures is still high when these devices are used by inexperienced, panic-stricken hikers. Even the best snakebite kits claim to remove only 30 percent of the venom, and only that if the device is used within three minutes. Given the low risk faced by a healthy adult, it seems best for most victims to let the problem run its course.

LIGHTNING

Every year, lightning kills 100 to 300 Americans. Only a handful are backpackers; the rest are mountaineers, golfers, boaters, swimmers and others.

Intense thunderstorms generate lightning by a mechanism that is still poorly understood, although it is known that the difference in electrical potential between the ends of a lightning stroke may reach hundreds of millions of volts. When lightning flashes, the air along its path is heated momentarily to perhaps 27,000°. The heated air expands explosively, causing thunder. Sound travels about one mile every five seconds, so the interval between a lightning flash and the sound of thunder tells you the distance to the storm. If lightning is frequent, keep track of the time between a lightning bolt and its thunderclap. If the time is decreasing, the storm is approaching you. *Find shelter immediately.*

Thunderstorms are characterized by violent updrafts within the storm itself that can reach 60 mph. Rapid condensation created as the updraft cools is the cause of a thunderstorm's pounding rain. When the rising air tops out at the top of the cloud, it cascades down the outside of the storm and spreads out along the ground, creating the sudden, cool breeze that heralds a thunderstorm's arrival. Severe thunderstorms can be distinguished from less violent ones by the size, shape, and position of the cloud. Cumulus clouds with low bases should be watched carefully. The low base indicates air with abundant moisture that needs to cool only a little to begin condensing. Anvil-

IF CAUGHT IN THE OPEN BY A LIGHTENING
STORM, KNEEL ON YOUR PACK AND WAIT
TILL IT PASSES.

shaped thunderstorms have updrafts powerful enough to reach the upper limit of the troposphere, which is several miles high. Overshooting thunderstorms, in which the normally flat top of the anvil bulges, are more dangerous still.

Prevention is obviously better than treatment when confronted with an immensely powerful force of nature like lightning. Lightning most often strikes tall, isolated objects—a peak, a rocky spire, a single tree in a meadow—or a person standing in an open area. If a thunderstorm threatens, get off the summits and ridges. If a dense forest is nearby, plunge in and relax—you're safe. Stay away from isolated trees and clumps of trees; they can act as lightning rods. If you are caught in the open with nowhere to hide, set metal objects such as tent poles, ice axes, and tripods aside and move several hundred yards away. Kneel down and put your hands on your knees. The idea is to reduce your height to the extent possible to avoid acting as a lightning rod, yet to minimize your contact with the ground so that the ground current set up by a lightning strike has the smallest possible avenue to enter your body. If possible, crouch on an insulator, like a pack or a climbing rope. Ground currents caused by lightning tend to flow along the paths taken by the rain as it runs off cliffs or hillsides. Shallow caves and overhanging rocks don't necessarily offer good protection from ground currents, which can flow along the cave walls or arc across the cave's mouth. A person hit by lightning frequently stops breathing. In addition, the victim's heart may stop beating. Be prepared to start cardiopulmonary resuscitation, a technique which requires specialized training in advance. Prompt CPR has saved the life of many lightning victims.

EMERGENCIES

What should you do if someone *really* gets hurt? The answer depends, in part, on the number of people in the group. A solo hiker can only shout and hope. A pair of hikers faces a difficult decision: should the uninjured member go for help, leaving behind a companion who may be unable to take care of himself? In both situations, you would have done yourself a favor if you had let someone responsible know where you were going and when you planned to be back. Most wilderness areas in the United States fall within the purview of some kind of organized search-and-rescue outfit. If you don't return on schedule, your friend can alert the authorities to come look for you. In some cases, the uninjured member of a team of two may be better off to sit tight, care for the injured member, and wait for rescuers than to try to make some heroic dash for help. Mountaineers on difficult climbs

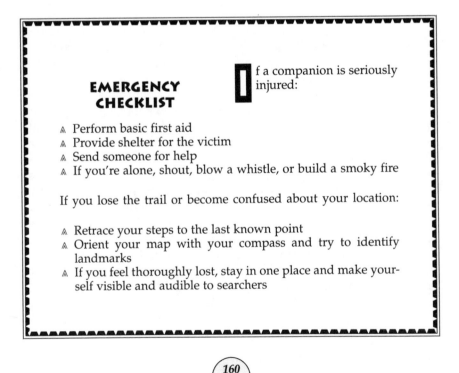

EMERGENCY CHECKLIST

If a companion is seriously injured:

⚠ Perform basic first aid
⚠ Provide shelter for the victim
⚠ Send someone for help
⚠ If you're alone, shout, blow a whistle, or build a smoky fire

If you lose the trail or become confused about your location:

⚠ Retrace your steps to the last known point
⚠ Orient your map with your compass and try to identify landmarks
⚠ If you feel thoroughly lost, stay in one place and make yourself visible and audible to searchers

frequently fall into this category. A group of three makes the problem easier; one person stays with the victim while the other goes out. Four is even better, because two people can head out together to get help, reducing the chance of another accident, while the third person stays with the victim.

Novices also fret over this question: what if I get lost? If you take the time to keep track of your position throughout the hike, you're very unlikely to get seriously off track. If the trail seems to peter out and vanish abruptly, stop and think. The usual cause of such an event is that you missed a turn in the trail a few hundred yards back. Retrace your steps and look for where you might have gone wrong. (You were looking over your shoulder periodically so you could easily retrace your steps, right?) You may need to hike all the way back to the last point you can positively identify on the map and start over again from there. If nothing seems familiar as you try to retrace your steps, get out the map and compass, orient the map, and try to identify some landmarks. From these, you should be able to determine your location.

If all else fails, sit down. Think about what could have gone wrong. Have a bite to eat. Food can have a very calming effect. Make noise. Perhaps someone will hear you. The odds are good that two parties didn't manage to get lost simultaneously in exactly the same spot. The other group can probably tell you where you are. Above all else, don't panic, pick a direction at random, and blunder ahead, hoping to stumble across something familiar. You're all too likely to leave the area that searchers will concentrate on, making their task much more difficult. Instead, wait for rescuers to find you. If you can, make yourself visible to searchers on the ground and in the air. Spread out a brightly colored garment, sleeping bag or tent in the middle of a meadow. Keep your group together to combine your strengths and to boost morale.

For most backpackers, the question of what to do in a real emergency remains hypothetical throughout their lives. In more than twenty years of wilderness travel, I have never even come close to feeling hopelessly lost. If you follow the precautions outlined in this book, you will almost certainly build the same track record. I have also been fortunate to be a witness to only a few accidents, all of which involved rock-climbing and mountaineering, not backpacking. Treat the wilderness with the respect it deserves, and you'll be able to travel safely in it for a lifetime.

WINTER: THE COOL ADVENTURE

> "Most of the luxuries, and many of the so-called comforts of life, are not only not indispensable, but positive hindrances to the elevation of mankind."
>
> —Henry Thoreau, *Walden*

Joe and I could hear the deep roar of the trucker's brakes on Interstate 70 as we stepped into our ski bindings, shouldered our packs, and plunged into the winter wilderness of the Gore Range. Behind us, immediately adjacent to the four-lane highway, lay Vail, one of the nation's biggest and most popular alpine ski resorts. Ahead of us lay miles of untracked white and the jagged 13,000-foot peaks of the Eagles Nest Wilderness. We saw no people as we started up the trail. There were no other cars in the parking lot, although it was merely a quarter of a mile from the interstate; the lot's miniscule size indicated that very few cars were expected. Half an hour after we began, the old ski tracks we were following vanished and we were on our own, with no sign of human presence. Four days later, as we emerged on the far side of the range, we finally encountered another person—a rancher inspecting his herd.

I've traversed the Gore Range in winter twice since then. Both times, I've seen no one. Not all Colorado ranges are quite that empty. Still, in comparison to summer, winter is the season of silence and peace in the high country so long as you seek out the places where snowmobiles are banned. For example, backcountry use in Rocky Mountain National Park from October 1 to May 1—two-thirds of the year—is less than 10 percent of the year's total. The lack of people pressure and the protection provided to the land by the carpet of snow allows rangers to relax the restrictions on where you can camp. In Rocky Mountain National Park, for example, you can pitch a tent anywhere you want if there's 4 inches of snow on the ground. If you want to get away from people, go to the high mountains when they're blanketed with snow.

Even in the lowlands, below the snow line, winter is usually the off-season. By Thanksgiving, if not sooner, the crowds have thinned considerably from the lemminglike hordes of summer. Snow-phobic backpackers will find that the cold months are a fine time to explore the southern tier of states and the Pacific and Atlantic coasts. Winter can be a wonderful time to hike in the desert Southwest, although I remember one New Year's trip to Utah's Arches National Park when the temperature dipped to 0 every night and the daytime highs were only in the 20s. Backpacking below the snow line in winter is only a little different from summer backpacking. A few extra layers of clothing and perhaps a warmer sleeping bag are all that is really needed. To fully savor the season, however, backpackers should venture into the high mountains of New England and the West, where winter truly reigns supreme. Winter backcountry travelers there must be prepared to deal with snow.

TRAVELING IN SNOW COUNTRY

Early in the fall, when the first snows are sifting down, it's usually still possible—if occasionally laborious—to travel without the aid of snowshoes or skis. You'll need warm, waterproof boots, and gaiters to keep snow out of your boot tops. Snow that is but a few inches deep will slow your pace only slightly as your feet grope for a solid purchase under the white velvet blanket. Ski poles or a walking stick can help steady your stride. As the snow deepens, you'll find yourself postholing, the hiker's nickname for plunging in to your knees with every step. Deep postholing can exhaust the strongest hiker in short order. By the time the snow, on average, is deeper than mid-calf, it's time to learn to walk on water—frozen, fluffy water, that is.

Snowshoes are much easier to use than cross-country skis. Most people master the ducklike waddle required within a few minutes. Although some people disdain them, I find ski poles reduce the number of times I trip over my newly acquired webbed feet. Snowshoes are also much less expensive than the kind of cross-country ski equipment you need to carry a substantial pack in the backcountry. For snowshoeing footwear, you can use a pair of inexpensive pac boots, which have a molded rubber bottom, stitched leather or nylon top and some kind of felt liner. The smallest models of snowshoes work well, even with an overnight-size pack, if you'll be traveling on routes where skiers or other snowshoers are likely to have broken trail. If you're trying to break trail yourself, however, small snowshoes will sometimes let you plunge in to your waist. You can either take that as a sign that you've lost favor with the Almighty or that you've encountered the rotten sugar-snow conditions common during some seasons in the Rockies and elsewhere. Supplication and/or medium-to-large snowshoes are essential under those circumstances.

Skis are a much more glamorous method of snow-country travel than snowshoes. Unfortunately, skiing with a big pack in fickle, unpredictable backcountry snow while using supple cross-country boots attached to the ski only at the toe is vastly different from film makers' celluloid fantasies. If your skiing experience is limited to schussing down beautifully manicured slopes at a posh resort while wearing combat equipment—stiff, high-backed boots locked down to wide, stable alpine skis—then your first venture into the backcountry may be, quite literally, a frigid plunge. In fact, there was many a time when I was learning to ski with a pack when I swore through clenched teeth that I could *walk* down the blasted slope faster than I could ski it. Even experienced skiers can be defeated by heavy loads, steep slopes, and tight slots through dense trees.

Despite these dire warnings, I must admit that I much prefer to bring skis rather than snowshoes. Even after eighteen years of skiing, I still find it exhilarating when the trail snakes down through the woods at a moderate pitch and I can simply stand on my skis as the pine trees swish by, traveling almost effortlessly toward my destination. Viewed rightly, difficult snow conditions and steep terrain can be an enjoyable challenge and the inevitable falls an occasion for a good laugh, not an oath. But I must confess that this saintly attitude deserts me on occasion when I fall twice for every successful turn.

When buying your first set of cross-country ski gear, avoid the mistake I made. I chose the flimsiest possible low-cut boots and lightweight skis without metal edges that were more suitable for touring on a snow-covered golf course than for tackling the Colorado high country. The result was that I floundered for years until two friends who owned a ski shop gently suggested that I might actually learn to ski someday if I invested in some decent equipment. As a minimum, buy yourself solidly built boots that are high enough to cover your anklebones and skis with metal edges, so that you have a fighting chance when the trails get scrapped off and icy. You should also pick up a pair of skins to attach to the bottom of your skis for steep uphill sections. Skins are made of a furry synthetic material that allows your skis to slide forward but prevents them from sliding back. They save a tremendous amount of energy on long climbs when compared to using waxes to provide your skis with grip. Some people leave their skins on during difficult descents to slow themselves down. However, I find that wearing skins when skiing downhill causes a jerky gait in which the skis grab one moment, then slide forward the next. In my opinion, that's worse than having a predictable—if fast—surface on the bottom of my skis.

I have a secret to share with those who love backcountry skiing so much that ski gear is a higher priority than a TV, a VCR, or next week's groceries. Backcountry skiers don't need to resign themselves to being Nordic nerdics performing telemark turns with one cross-country ski pushed well ahead of the other. Backcountry skiers can now bring the control of alpine skis and the flexibility of touring skis into the backcountry with hybrid boots, bindings and skis collectively called alpine-touring equipment. Alpine-touring boots are high-backed and stiff, just like alpine boots, but they have a lever above the heel that lets you adjust the amount of forward lean. With the lever in one position, the boots force your lower leg forward, just like alpine boots. With the lever in the other position, the boots allow an upright stance suitable for walking and touring. The bindings are similarly

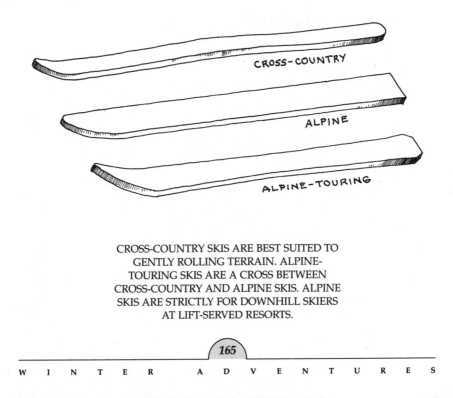

CROSS-COUNTRY SKIS ARE BEST SUITED TO
GENTLY ROLLING TERRAIN. ALPINE-
TOURING SKIS ARE A CROSS BETWEEN
CROSS-COUNTRY AND ALPINE SKIS. ALPINE
SKIS ARE STRICTLY FOR DOWNHILL SKIERS
AT LIFT-SERVED RESORTS.

Janus-like: in the locked-down configuration, they let you clamp your heel to the ski for maximum control on the downhill run just like alpine bindings. In the touring configuration, the bindings allow your heel to rise and fall while you walk just like standard three-pin cross-country bindings. Like alpine skis, alpine-touring skis are shorter and wider than cross-country skis. Unlike alpine skis, however, alpine-touring skis are relatively light, so they feel less like lead ankle weights when you are climbing a hill.

For me, the purchase of alpine-touring equipment opened up a whole new world. Suddenly it became possible to actually *ski* instead of merely survive while carrying an overnight pack. For the first time I could contemplate skiing off the summits of high peaks (with due consideration being given to avalanche danger). True, alpine-touring gear has its limitations. It's heavier than ordinary cross-country equipment, close to twice as expensive, and cumbersome to use in rolling terrain where you might feel the need to switch frequently from locked-down to touring mode. On flat ground, using alpine-touring gear is a slog. In most parts of Yellowstone, for example, alpine-touring equipment would be an expensive encumbrance. In much of the Colorado Rockies, however, where you're usually either climbing steadily or making a long continuous run back down, it's perfect. If you're a good alpine skier and want to be able to use your existing technique in rugged backcountry rather than trying to master the telemark turn, alpine-touring gear may be the way to go.

WINTER SHELTERS

The summer tent you have been using will probably work fine for many winter excursions if you take care to pitch it below the timberline in dense forest so that it's not battered by high winds. You will also need to shovel snow off the roof after a heavy snowfall to prevent the roof from sagging and possibly breaking a pole. If your winter adventures get more serious, you will want to invest in a winter tent, probably a dome with four interlocking poles that will stand up to high winds and heavy snow loads. Chapter 5 gives more details on desirable features.

Start preparing a winter tent site by stamping out a level platform with boots, skis or snowshoes. Give the platform a few minutes to harden after you are done stamping to help prevent your knees and elbows from punching big depressions in the tent platform when you crawl inside your tent. You don't want to feel as if you're sleeping in a bathtub or, worse yet, atop a series of irregularly spaced buckets. Sometimes tent-pole segments can't be connected in exceptionally cold weather because the shock cord running through the segments freezes in elongated form. The excess cord protruding from the ends of the pole segments prevents the segments from being joined. If you encounter this problem, pull on the shock cord rapidly and repeatedly. Usually this will warm the cord just enough that it will regain its elasticity and allow the pole segments to be connected. Conventional tent pegs don't work in the snow, of course, so you'll need to find substitute anchors. Skis, ski poles, and snowshoes all work well if you are going to be taking down the tent before you need that equipment again. If you plan to set up a base camp and leave the tent erect while you take day trips, try anchoring your tent to stuff sacks that you have filled with snow and buried.

Some people prefer to leave the tent at home and dig snow caves instead. In severe weather, snow caves offer several advantages: they are impervious to wind, and they are also warmer and quieter than a tent because the snow acts as an insulator. Most caves will warm up to near freezing after they've been occupied for a while. Despite these appealing aspects, snow caves also leave a lot to be desired. Digging a snow cave is a hard, wet job that can easily consume two or three hours. Finding a suitable site can be difficult, since the snow must be both deep and sufficiently consolidated. I have dug snow caves in near-emergency situations in Alaska when high winds threatened our

A CROSS SECTION OF A SNOW CAVE.

tents. In those situations, I blessed the security the caves provided. In general, however, I prefer to carry the weight of a tent, which in good weather admits more light and is much warmer than a snow cave. A light-colored tent can act as a greenhouse on a sunny day. The warmth boosts morale and helps dry sodden gear, which will actually dry faster inside the tent than it will draped over the roof outside. When the sun is shining, crawling into a snow cave is like entering a walk-in refrigerator.

Backcountry skiers who want to continue making multi-day excursions in the winter but who can't stand the idea of sleeping in the cold should investigate the possibility of staying in a backcountry hut or yurt. Over the past ten years, several immensely popular chains of huts have blossomed in the Colorado backcountry. One of the most heavily used systems is the group of ten huts operated by the Tenth Mountain Division Trail Association in the triangle between Leadville, Aspen and Vail. (See the appendix for the address and phone number.) Demand is so heavy that reservations must be made the previous summer for the popular weekends. These huts are equipped with wood heating stoves, propane cooking stoves, mattresses, and a photovoltaic system that powers energy-efficient electric lights. Skiers bring their own food and lightweight sleeping bags. Call your local outdoor shop to find out what huts may exist in your area.

CAMPING IN WINTER

Probably the biggest worry of newcomers to the winter backcountry is that they'll get cold. In reaction to this apparently logical fear, they often get out of the car, bundle up in six layers of clothing, and head up the trail. Within fifteen minutes, sweat is dripping from their earlobes. When they stop moving, evaporation from their sweat-soaked clothes immediately chills them right down to their cotton underwear. In their attempt to avoid getting cold, they actually have made the problem worse.

Even more than in the summer, the key to remaining comfortable is to take the time to adjust clothing as soon as your temperature starts to feel out of balance. Pause to shed clothing before you start dripping. Add a layer before you start to shiver. Carry synthetic clothing that dries fast and doesn't absorb sweat. Select clothing that can be ventilated easily. I prefer jackets with full zippers rather than pullovers for this reason. I also like pile pants and shell pants with full side zippers that allow me to ventilate even while I'm moving. It's even better if the zippers separate completely into two halves when they're unzipped. Picture someone trying to pull on a pair of blue jeans while wearing skis, and you'll understand the value of full separating side zippers, which allow you to put on your pants without taking off your skis or snowshoes. For a full treatise on the art of staying warm in cold weather, see my book *Cold Comfort*, published by Lyons & Burford.

If you get serious about winter camping, you'll probably want to buy a full-on winter sleeping bag. (See Chapter 6 for details on what to look for.)

In the wintertime, every minute you spend thinking about the details before the trip is one less minute you'll spend cursing the details once you're out in the cold. For example, the slider on every zipper on your pack, outer clothing, and tent should be equipped with a short loop of stout cord so you can manipulate the zipper without removing your gloves. In a similar fashion, look for ways to modify your tent so that it can be pitched with gloves on. For example, I drilled holes through the ends of the tent poles for a Stephenson tent I own and tied loops of cord through them so I could grab them effectively with gloved hands. Avoid buttons on winter clothing—you'll need bare hands to manipulate them. Trying to button your shirt while wearing gloves is like trying to eat beef broth with chopsticks. Snaps are a little better, but zippers are best once they're equipped with zipper pulls. Velcro-closed pockets are often annoying because the Velcro either grabs your gloves (if you're wearing them) or scratches your bare hands, which are usually already sensitized by the cold. One more tip: try storing your water bottle upside down in your pack so that any ice that forms won't cause the cap to freeze shut. The prerequisite for this trick, of course, is finding a water bottle that absolutely does not leak.

Once you have got the tent pitched, start the stove immediately. You'll probably have to melt snow to obtain water, and that takes a long time. To keep your hot stove from sinking into the snow and tipping over, bring a small square of thin plywood and set your stove atop it. Cover the plywood with a thin piece of sheet metal. Some stoves run so hot that they can ignite the plywood if it's left unprotected. Take care in handling white gas in cold weather. It remains liquid at very low temperatures and can easily cause frostbite if it is spilled on unprotected skin.

AVALANCHES

Avalanches are probably the most fearsome hazard in the winter backcountry because they are both lethal and unpredictable. Everyone who travels in the high country in winter should take an avalanche seminar such as those offered by the American Avalanche Institute and various search-and-rescue groups. What follows is merely the basics.

Avalanches are most common on slopes ranging from 30° to 45° in steepness, but they can occur even on more gentle slopes when conditions are very unstable. They occur most frequently on slopes that are heavily loaded with snow by the wind. Wind-scoured, west-facing slopes are generally safer than east-facing slopes, where that wind-scoured snow is subsequently deposited. Cornices—overhanging wavelike formations—frequently form at the top of dangerous wind-loaded slopes. Avalanches can be triggered by the collapse of a cornice, by the addition of snow to a slope by wind or a snowstorm, or by the weight of a skier or snowshoer. Many avalanches run during and immediately after large storms. Gullies and broad concave bowls accumulate snow and are therefore more dangerous than ridges, where the snowpack is usually more shallow. However, travelers on ridges should take care not to walk on top of cornices, which can collapse under their weight. Not all steep slopes will avalanche if you ski them, but predicting which ones will slide and which won't is nearly impossible. A trained observer can gain some clues by digging a snow pit and examining the layers in the snow pack, but digging a pit and then deciding to ski a slope because you think it's safe is like betting your life on a fortune-teller's reading of tea leaves.

To avoid avalanches, stay off open slopes between 30° and 45°. Widely scattered trees will not necessarily protect you. To be safe from avalanches, a forest must have trees that are spaced too closely to provide enjoyable skiing. Give avalanche runout zones a wide berth. Avalanches that have fallen a considerable distance build up enough momentum to travel for long distances on flat ground.

Finally, listen for warning signs. An unstable snowpack, even on level ground, will frequently settle with an ominous whompf! under the weight of your skis. The sound is caused by the collapse of weak layers in the snowpack. If you hear the snowpack settle, exercise even greater caution than normal.

WINTER WEATHER

In the continental United States in winter, bad weather is usually produced by major low-pressure systems tracking west to east. If your trip will last only a couple of days, you should be able to get a decent weather forecast before you start. The National Weather Service, with its far-flung network of observing stations, will always be able to do a much better job of predicting the weather than you will by observing conditions in your immediate vicinity. However, a knowledge of the typical pattern of clouds generated by an approaching low-pressure system can be helpful, particularly if you're out for several days and the forecast you got at the beginning of the trip has become outdated.

About 24 to 48 hours before a storm hits, high cirrus clouds usually began to cover the sky. These feathery or fibrous clouds are composed of ice crystals and found above 23,000 feet. As the storm draws closer, the cirrus thicken to cirrostratus, a more continuous, sheetlike cloud that often causes a halo around the sun or moon. Stratus means stratified or layered. This sequence of cirrus followed by cirrostratus is important, for cirrus alone is not necessarily a sign of bad weather. As the storm gets closer, the cirrostratus lower and thicken further to altostratus, layered middle-level clouds between 6,500 and 23,000 feet. When the storm is imminent, the altostratus thickens and descends to form nimbostratus, a continuous blanket of low-level (below 6,500 feet) clouds, and snow begins to fall. Low-pressure systems less than 300 miles across usually die out within 36 hours. Bigger ones, from 350 to 1,800 miles across, often last three or four days. This idealized portrait of a low-pressure system doesn't correspond perfectly to every storm you'll encounter, but at least it gives you some clues on what to look for.

SPRINGTIME

Springtime may be my favorite time in the high mountains. The scenery still says winter, but the weather says spring. The avalanche danger has both diminished and become far more predictable. As the snowpack consolidates and stabilizes under the influence of the warm spring sun, the breakable crust of midwinter gives way to delightful corn snow, the world's easiest snow to ski. Very few people come to the mountains then, because there is a bit of a catch: you have to be willing to get up early.

Warm days and still-cold nights mean that the snowpack goes through a strong daily cycle. At dawn the snowpack is usually frozen hard enough to bear a skier's weight, so travel is fast and easy. By mid-morning, the surface has softened to a depth of an inch or so, and downhill runs are silken perfection. By noon the snow has softened still further and skiing has become more difficult as skiers must force their skis to turn in deep slush. The avalanche danger begins to climb. By mid-afternoon, liquid water is percolating through the snowpack, loosening the bonds that hold the snowpack's layers together, and the avalanche danger is climbing to unacceptable levels. Even on the flats, travel can be difficult as skis plunge into the rotten snowpack. After sunset, the snowpack begins to refreeze, and at dawn the cycle repeats itself. The key to enjoying springtime travel and to avoiding avalanches, therefore, is to adopt Ben Franklin's motto: early to bed, early to rise, makes a man healthy, wealthy and alive.

The information contained here is only a primer on what you need to know to travel safely and comfortably in the high mountains in the snowy months. What's said of life in general is particularly true of winter camping: good judgment comes from experience, and experience comes from bad judgment. Winter places far greater demands on fitness, route-finding skills, camping techniques and the ability to take care of yourself in foul weather than summer does. Even with the best gear, the discomfort quotient is undeniably higher. In the winter, even more than in the summer, the wilderness demands respect. Despite the many problems, however, winter travel in the high mountains is an experience that many find far more rewarding than cruising up some summertime wilderness highway masquerading as a trail and pulling into a designated backcountry campsite. In its solitary character and confrontation with nature in the raw, it is an experience far closer to what most people imagine wilderness travel should be like. It should not be missed.

BACKPACKING WITH CHILDREN

"Let children walk with nature, let them see the beautiful blendings and communions of death and life, their joyous inseparable unity, as taught in woods and meadows, plains and mountains and streams of our blessed star, and they will learn that death is stingless indeed, and as beautiful as life, and that the grave has no victory, for it never fights. All is divine harmony."

—John Muir, *A Thousand-mile Walk to the Gulf*, 1916

iking with children is far different from exploring the backcountry with other adults. To their credit, children are rarely as obsessed with goals as their parents. They cannot fathom the notion of hiking nonstop for hours with eyes fixated on Dad's boot heels in order to reach some scenic vista. Instead, kids are interested in the little things right in front of them. They love to inspect the bugs, beetles, lizards, and leaves that line the trail. While backpacking in Rocky Mountain National Park with our neighbors Gregg and Amy

Thayer, their daughters Maggie and Jessie became fascinated with renaming the flowers they encountered. The game occupied them for an entire mile—a long time for two young children. Kids don't comprehend why Daddy and Mommy, with their massive packs, are eager to cover the miles as quickly as possible so that they can drop their loads for the last time, and they don't grasp why adults don't share their fascination with the minute wonders that spring into view at every step. As the Little Prince put it in Antoine de Saint-Exupéry's novel of the same name, "Grownups never understand anything for themselves, and it is tiresome for children to be always and forever explaining things to them."

Before taking your kids into the wilderness, make sure that you yourself feel comfortable there. Don't try to learn how to pitch your tent and fire up your stove when you've got cold, hungry, tired kids in tow. Even experts should never go into the woods as the only adult with young children. If something should happen to the adult, the whole group could be in serious trouble. Two adults are a minimum. Ideally, the ratio of adults to children under seven should be one to one. At worst, there should be one adult for every two children.

THE STAGES OF A WILDERNESS CHILDHOOD

In some ways, infants are easier to take into the woods, at least for a day hike, than children of any other age. By comparison to older kids, infants are very portable and require minimal additional equipment. Up until the age of eight months or a year, infants ride comfortably in a soft chest pack. When infants outgrow the chest pack, they enjoy riding on a parent's back in a child pack with a soft nylon seat and a rigid aluminum frame. Lou Dawson, the first person to ski all 54 of Colorado's 14,000-foot peaks, used to take his one-year-old son Louie with him in a child pack when he trained by skiing up, then down, the slopes of Ski Sunlight, an alpine resort near his home in Carbondale, Colorado. Needless to say, Lou was extremely confident that he would not fall. Louie never complained, and in fact seemed to enjoy it.

In either kind of pack, infants need to be bundled up more warmly than you, since they aren't active. They also need protection from the sun and from mosquitoes and other biting insects. Don't apply sunscreen or insect repellent to areas that an infant might suck. One maker of child packs offers as an accessory an awning that attaches to the pack frame and shades the occupant. With the addition of a little mosquito netting, the awning would serve to keep bugs off as well. Child packs that hold children high let them see better, which

UP TO THE AGE OF EIGHT MONTHS OR A
YEAR, MOST INFANTS RIDE COMFORTABLY
IN A CHEST PACK.

may keep them happier. They also position children where they can easily yank on a parent's hair, and where their screams have the maximum effect on a parent's tattered nerves. One study showed that a baby screaming in a parent's arms actually sounded louder to the parent than a jackhammer at 10 feet. Fortunately, babies in child packs often sleep soundly for much of the ride, so, with luck, you won't be able to confirm the results of the study.

Life grows more complicated when a child begins to crawl, then walk. Many parents feel that the ages between two and four are the most difficult for taking children into the wilderness. No longer are kids content to ride for hours in a child pack. They want to get down and walk, but they really can't—or won't—walk very far. The same child that will scamper about a playground for hours, displaying enough energy to power New York in a blackout, will walk a hundred yards on a trail and begin asking, "When are we going to get there?" The difference, say expert parents, is that the playground provides an exciting series of immediate diversions, while the designated campsite seems impossibly far away. The key to motivating a child on the trail, therefore, is to provide a tantalizing series of nearby goals: counting the pine cones under the big ponderosa a hundred yards up the trail, then examining the stream you can hear around the bend for tadpoles and water skeeters. My Mom and Dad used M&Ms, doled out in small handfuls every 20 or 30 minutes, to entice me and Amy up the trail.

Some kids are easier to motivate than others. Cora and I took a 3-mile hike once with two nephews. Micah was two and Izaac was four. Micah, a sturdy little chap, strode along happily for most of the way, while his older brother hung back complaining and finally insisted on being carried in an ordinary day pack even though the cramped foot area put his legs to sleep. I felt as if I was carrying a sack of squirming potatoes, but Izaac was happy and the rest of the hike went smoothly.

By the age of four, many kids will want to carry their own little day pack containing, at most, a sweater and a favorite snack. Even this minuscule load will often end up on Mommy or Daddy's back before the day—or hour—is out. Outings should be short, a few miles at the most, and parents should remember that the fun limit may be much less than the actual physical limit. One mistake my parents made was doing too much the first day. They recall one time in particular when I was five. The first day we walked to the top of Sequoia's Moro Rock, which provided a fine view of the Kaweah River valley. The 3-mile hike so wore me out, however, that I collapsed into bed immediately after breakfast the next day and refused to move until noon. Be prepared to provide entertainment during the frequent stops you will make. Snacks and juice have entertainment as well as nutritional value. Make up games as you go along, or sing songs, or tell stories.

By the time children reach seven or eight, they're probably ready for a child-size internal- or external-frame pack. In the past, finding such a pack was difficult to impossible. Fortunately for outdoorsy parents, baby boomers are having kids in sufficient numbers now that several companies have found it profitable to produce decent kid's packs. When selecting one, look for the maximum possible amount of adjustability in the torso length, the distance between the waist belt and the point where the shoulder straps attach to the pack bag or pack frame. As with all children's equipment and clothing, you want gear that can be adjusted to fit a growing body for as long as possible.

A child's load on a backpacking trip should be about one-fourth of his or her body weight. Some kids can carry a little more, others a little less. With a bit of luck and a lot of cajoling, you should be able to get them to carry their own pint-size sleeping bag and most of their clothes.

Before the age of seven or eight, most kids can get by on dry trails with sneakers. Once they start carrying a pack with significant weight, however, you should consider buying them a pair of children's hiking boots. One clever company sells boots with a peel-off innersole that can be removed to accommodate growing feet. With any pair of boots, fit them initially with two or even three pairs of socks, then gradually reduce the sock thickness as the child's feet grow. Parents should check their kid's feet periodically for hot spots. Reddened skin should be covered immediately with moleskin to prevent a blister from forming. Kids usually don't complain about their feet until a full-grown blister has erupted, so it's up to you to forestall trouble.

At some point in the teenage years, your children's strength and stamina, which is on the rise, will surpass yours, which is on the decline. At that longed-for point you may actually be able to ask them to shoulder more than half the load. By that time, unfortunately, they'll probably prefer going off with friends their own age.

CAMPING WITH KIDS

At any age, day-hiking with children is easier than backpacking with them. On a day-hike, if the weather turns sour or a child suddenly gets sick, the car is usually just a short distance away. If a similar situation develops on a backpacking trip, the time required to get out is much greater. Backpacking is also more difficult than day-hiking because of the dramatic increase in the parent's load. Parent's packs are heavy with an oversize tent, extra food, and most of the kid's clothing and gear. Dawdling along at a child's inchworm pace can be torture when you've got a monster pack on your back.

If the child is too young to walk, then one parent must carry the babe in a child pack while the other totes the remaining gear. Usually the sheer bulk of the necessary equipment overwhelms the largest pack on the market, which means that two trips are necessary for the parent acting as educated alpine mule. That's feasible only if the campsite is just a mile or two from the trail head. An alternative to ferrying loads is to hire a teenager to act as a porter. Once the party reaches camp, the teenager can help baby-sit.

If backpacking with an infant sounds like lot of work, you're right. Nonetheless, it can be done. My neighbors Gregg and Amy, who are both ex-wilderness guides, started backpacking with their two daughters when the youngest was still in diapers. Still, you don't see many couples on the trail with children who are not yet potty trained. Cloth diapers can be washed out and reused if the weather is warm enough to permit airdrying and you bring along a separate diaper-washing pot. Wash water should always be dumped well away from any water source. If you bring disposables, you'll have to pack them out inside several layers of plastic bags.

Children like the familiar, and the wilderness can seem like a strange and intimidating place to a young child. Initially, at least, a tent doesn't seem like home, and children may find it difficult to go to sleep. To help alleviate those night fears, pitch your tent in your backyard and spend a night or two there before you go on a real backpacking trip. Children who like to sleep with a night light may find that a tent pitched in the wilderness seems awfully dark. To help relieve those fears, sit down with your children in the backyard and explain all the night noises they hear so they realize there's nothing to fear. Do the same once you're actually camping in the woods. Sometimes it helps to bring along a few favorite nighttime toys. Letting the kids help set up the tent familiarizes them with it and may make them more comfortable with sleeping inside it.

As a general rule, letting your child sleep with you inside your sleeping bag is an invitation to trouble. The child may sleep well, but you probably won't because the child's squirming will keep you awake. Each child should have his own sleeping bag, which shouldn't be more than about 4 inches longer than his height. A bag that is too big is hard to warm up, and the child is likely to sleep cold. Adequate child-size sleeping bags are available now. Look for a model with a hood that can be closed down snugly, just like an adult's. All children's sleeping bags have synthetic insulation, which in a kid's bag has the advantage over down that it can more easily be machine washed and dried.

If you have a choice of where to camp, try to select a site well away from other campers so the inevitable childish racket doesn't echo through the woods and disturb your neighbors. Check the site for obvious nearby hazards: a waterfall, a cliff, a patch of poison ivy or poison oak. Equally important, try to find a site with child appeal. Water, whether in the form of a pond or a stream, is always enticing. Equally good is a late-lingering snow patch, which provides endless ammunition for snowball fights and building material for snowmen and snow forts. Beware of snowfields that slope steeply and end abruptly in brush and boulders. A child can easily start sliding out of control and crash into the obstacles at the snowfield's foot.

Whether on the trail or in camp, parents should establish an absolute, unbendable rule that children will always play within sight of an adult. The cooking area and the tent should be ruled off-limits to play. Little fingers can too easily be burned on a hot stove or hot pots, and little feet can easily trip over tent pegs and guy ropes. Consider giving children a whistle and then making another rule: the whistle will be blown only in the case of a real emergency. An adult should accompany children when they need to go to the toileting area, which, as with adults, should be well away from any water source. Adult supervision ensures that the child doesn't wander off and that he buries his waste properly. Be sure your pack contains a well-stocked repair kit. Kids are hard on gear, both their own and community items like tents.

When it comes time to break camp, encourage your kids to help you police the site for any litter you may accidentally have dropped or that may have been left behind by previous campers. If need be, make it a game. Pretend you're trappers or Indians seeking to leave no trace of your passage so your enemies can't track you down. By teaching children at an early age about no-trace camping, you can be confident you'll be raising another responsible citizen of the wilderness.

INVESTING YOURSELF IN WILDERNESS FUTURES

"A man and what he loves and builds have but a day and then disappear; nature cares not—and renews the annual round untired. It is the old law, sad but not bitter. Only when man destroys the life and beauty of nature, there is the outrage."

—**George Macaulay Trevelyan,** *Grey of Fallodon,* **1937**

I well remember a scheme so outrageous that I couldn't believe anyone had seriously suggested it—yet someone had. A gravel company had proposed a tenfold expansion of a small but already troublesome quarry on Eldorado Mountain, near Boulder, Colorado. The operation would have devoured the entire northeastern flank of the mountain and left a scar 2,000 feet high—as big as the face of Half Dome in Yosemite National Park, 500 feet taller than Chicago's Sears Tower. Eldorado Mountain rises in the center of a broad complex of recreational land visited by 500,000 people every year.

For ten years, I had enjoyed the steep climbs that abound on the walls of nearby Eldorado Canyon. Eldorado Mountain graced the southwestern skyline every time I went running in Boulder's Mountain Parks. I immediately joined the newborn organization fighting the expansion. Together we wrote flyers and raised the money to print and mail them. We assembled a slide show and spoke to civic organizations large and small. We took our message to planning boards, city councils and county commissioners. In the end, we won a unanimous verdict of opposition to the expanded quarry from every government body with jurisdiction. After months of negotiations, Boulder bought the company's lease. The quarry shut down, and Eldorado Mountain seemed safe.

Safe, that is, until some California company unearthed an obscure federal law and began an attempt to build a water-power project on Eldorado Mountain's southern flanks. The city immediately mobilized to fight this inane project, which would consume more energy than it produced and make money only because the power generated could be sold during daylight hours, when electricity rates are at their peak. Fortunately, the company canceled the project when the strength of the opposition became apparent.

Organized, aroused citizens *can* make a difference. Our efforts helped preserve wildlife habitat, healthy watershed and recreational opportunities that will grow more valuable with each passing year. Sadly enough, however, most environmental victories require constant vigilance to remain secure. Conservationists need more than powerful lungs. They need stamina, too.

The United States is the fourth largest country on earth. Its boundaries encompass 3.6 million square miles, an area almost as big as Europe. Today only about 4 percent—149,000 square miles—has been protected as wilderness under the terms of the 1964 Wilderness Act. Even that number is deceptive, since nearly two-thirds of America's wilderness is concentrated in Alaska. In the Lower 48, only 2 percent of the land has been preserved in its pristine form. Many states have no wilderness whatsoever. The vast majority of America has already been plowed and paved and put to human use in a thousand ways. Surely we owe it to the other creatures great and small who inhabit this land with us to leave a little undisturbed for their benefit. Surely we owe it to ourselves to save some scraps of land where we can escape the din of machinery and the oppressive crush of the crowd.

Proof of how much people value wilderness can be found in the long lead times required to reserve a wilderness campsite in many of our national parks. The number of visitors to national parks and Forest Service and Bureau of Land Management recreation areas rises almost every year. America's ongoing love affair with the wilderness is also one of the chief threats to wilderness. This book has spent much time detailing these internal threats and what you can do to reduce the impact of your presence. Equally important, however, are the external threats. All national parks and wilderness areas will suffer if development is allowed just outside the wilderness boundaries. Few parks and wilderness areas preserve complete ecosystems. They depend for their biological health on a buffer zone of undeveloped or lightly developed land around them. Logging, mining, oil and gas production, off-road vehicles, excessive grazing, and urban sprawl all threaten these buffer zones.

It's time to draw boundaries around civilization instead of around wilderness. The number of human beings that the planet can sustain at our present levels of consumption is limited. We must find a way to construct a sustainable economy based on the resources we have already diverted to human use. In the long run, pillaging what little wilderness remains will do nothing to help.

If you love the wilderness and the opportunities it provides to hike and camp, if you value its role as a reservoir of biological diversity, if the thought of its silent beauty cheers you even when you're a thousand miles away, speak up. Start by becoming informed. Scan your local newspaper for items on environmental controversies. If you live in the West, subscribe to *High Country News*, one of the best sources of information on environmental issues affecting the region. The address is in the appendix. Join one or more of the major conservation organizations and read their magazines and newsletters. Environmentalists will never have the clout of major corporations unless they band together. Seek out the small local organizations that often do the most to solve local problems, or found an organization of your own. Write letters to your local newspaper and your local, state and federal representatives. The literature from conservation organizations will tell you which issues are hot and on which officials to exert public pressure. It's easy to be complacent, to think that the present wilderness system is secure and sufficient for all time. In fact, the battle to preserve wilderness in the United States is not over. Another 141,000 square miles of undeveloped land deserve protection, according to the Wilderness Society. Add your voice to those who are demanding that more land be preserved. Your duties to the land do not end when you pick up a last bit of litter as you stride back into the parking lot. In fact, they have just begun.

APPENDICES

PERIODICALS

Backpacker is the most useful periodical for backpackers who want advice on where to go, what to buy, and what prized wilderness areas are currently under assault by loggers, miners, dam builders and developers. Write to:

> *Backpacker*
> Rodale Press
> 33 East Minor St.
> Emmaus, PA 18098

The best coverage of environmental issues in the West is *High Country News.*

> *High Country News*
> P.O. Box 1090
> Paonia, CO 81428

MAPS

Many outdoor and sporting goods shops carry topographic maps of their region. If you can't find what you're looking for locally, write to:

> USGS Map Sales
> Federal Center
> Box 25286
> Denver, CO 80225

You can call (303) 236-7477 to request a free order form and index for the state you're interested in, but all orders must be in writing.

To obtain topographic maps of selected areas printed on waterproof, tear-proof plastic, contact:

Trails Illustrated
P.O. Box 3610
Evergreen, CO 80439–3425
(303) 670-3457 or (800) 962-1643
Fax (303) 670-3644

Trails Illustrated will accept orders by phone, mail, or fax.

BACKCOUNTRY HUTS

One of the most extensive backcountry hut systems in the country is run by the Tenth Mountain Division Trail Association. Contact them at:

Tenth Mountain Division Trail Association
1280 Ute Avenue
Aspen, CO 81611
(303) 925-5775

PACKING LISTS

This is the checklist Cora and I use for summer backpacking trips in the Rockies. It's an idiosyncratic list which I'm sure you will modify as you gain experience.

Personal Equipment

- two pairs of socks
- one pair of boots
- long johns or tights
- mosquito pants
- mosquito shirt
- shorts
- T-shirt
- long-sleeved turtleneck
- synthetic sweatshirt
- synthetic sweater
- fleece ski hat

- sun hat
- light gloves
- rain pants
- rain jacket
- sunglasses
- large garbage bag
- paperback book (sometimes)
- headlamp with extra batteries and spare bulb
- bowl
- spoon
- mug

- Swiss Army knife
- sleeping bag
- Therm-A-Rest
- Therm-A-Rest chair
- pack
- tube of lip sunscreen
- two or more water bottles
- a few small plastic bags
- toothbrush, toothpaste, floss
- watch

Group Equipment

- tent with stakes
- stove
- 1–1/4 quart pot with pot grips
- lighters
- matches
- extra fuel
- food
- map(s)
- compass
- altimeter

- wilderness permit, Park Service sketch map showing location of campsite, parking permit (for dash)
- trowel
- first-aid kit: moleskin, cloth tape, Band-Aids, 4x4 gauze pads, Advil, Ace bandage, etc.

- repair kit: pole patch, ripstop tape, stove parts, etc.
- Potable Aqua
- toilet paper
- bottle of skin sunscreen
- 50 feet of cord

For your amusement, I've included my camera checklist. This is for fanatics only.

Camera gear

- Nikon F4 camera body
- three or four Nikon autofocus lenses (usually 20mm, 24mm, 35mm, 80-200mm zoom)
- lens hoods
- graduated neutral-density filters and holder
- polarizing filters
- flash
- flash meter
- tripod
- cable release
- film
- camera repair/cleaning kit
- extra batteries
- notebook and pen
- Computer printout showing bearing and time of sunrise, sunset, moonrise and moonset

For hut-to-hut cross-country ski trips, we leave behind the Therm-A-Rest, Therm-A-Rest chair, stove, fuel, bowl, spoon, 50 feet of cord, tent, mosquito pants, mosquito shirt, rain pants, and large plastic garbage bag. Then we add:

Personal Hut-to-Hut Skiing Gear

- pile pants
- shell pants designed for skiing with full side zips
- down jacket (for Cora)
- cross-country ski boots
- skis
- ski poles
- climbing skins for skis
- snow shovel
- avalanche beacon
- goggles
- heavy mittens
- heavy gloves

Group Gear

- antifog paste for goggles and sunglasses
- wax kit: waxes for different temperature snow, scrapers, cork
- ski-repair kit: spare cables and tools to install them, wire and pliers with wire cutters

INDEX

abrasion, 18, 21

abrasion resistance, 19, 30

air travel, 45–46

Alaska, 25, 37, 39, 51, 68, 92, 146, 156, 167–68

Alaska Range, 25, 59, 63, 64, 138

Alpine Aire dinners, 92

alpine tundra, 115, 122, 124

altimeters, 105

American Alpine Club, 156

American Avalanche Institute, 169

ankles: support of, 28, 29, 30, 33, 34, 36

Appalachian Mountains, 17

Appalachian Trail, 94

AquaSeal, 38

Arapaho Pass, 16

Arches N.P., 163

aurora watching, 33

avalanches, 169–70, 171

backpacking, 9–13, 25, 44, 101; boom in, 11, 121–23, 132; pleasures of, 9–11

back pain, 45, 47, 48

Ball, Jenny, 81–82

batteries, 81–83, 95

bears, 130, 139, 140–45

Bee Seal Plus, 38

bee stings, 156

belts, 18, 24; see also Compression belts; Hip belts

Bibler, Todd, 59–60

bicomponent fabrics, 19–20

bivouac sacks, 54

Biwell, 38

blisters, 28, 29, 34, 35, 150–51

Blue Ridge Mountains, 123

book packs, 13, 40–41

boot-patching compounds, 30

boots, 26, 28–38, 84, 112, 150–51; failure points, 30; fitting of, 34–37; hiking, 28–29; leather, 29–32, 33–34, 36–37, 38; and load factor 29, 30, 31, 35, 36–37; mountaineering, 36–37; overboots, 84; pac, 32, 33–34, 38, 164; repair of, 30; summer, 34; telemark, 28; waterproof, 114, 163; waterproofing of, 30–32; winter, 35

breathable fabrics, 21–24

bruises, 34

bushwhacking, 14, 51

butane cartridges, 46

cairns, 115–17

cameras, see Photography

Camp Cooking, 90

campfires, 53, 75, 128–29

camping, 171; low-impact, 12, 121–39, 179, 182; permits, 121–23; site selection, 123–28

Camping Gaz Bleuet 206, 79

camp shoes, 34, 84

Canada, 25

Canadian Rockies, 53

Canyonlands N.P., 132

canyons, 34, 51, 112–13, 120

carbon monoxide poisoning, 145–46

car break-ins, 139

Carey, Cindy, 81–82

child packs, 174–75

children, 50, 173–79

cigarette lighters, 84

clevis pins, 85–86

cliffs, 34, 161

climbing, 10, 14, 42, 161

clothing, 16–27, 42, 46, 50, 53, 153; care of, 27; layering of, 20–21, 154; wicking in, 18, 19–20; see also indiv. items

Coleman stoves, 78

compass use, 13, 104–8, 109, 116, 159

compression straps, 41–42, 51

condensation, 58–60, 134, 138

Continental Divide, 28

cooking, 26, 58, 60, 128, 144, 146–47

Cordura nylon, 51, 150

corn snow, 171

Cotter, Lisa, 81–82

cotton, 17, 18, 19, 21, 35

CPR, 158

crampons, 38, 84
cryptogam soil, 124
Dawson, Lou, 174
day hiking, 13, 36, 113, 150
day packs, 13, 40–43
DEET, 149
Denali N.P., 144
desert hiking, 54, 85, 125, 130, 160–61
dogsled, 68
down garments, 17, 25, 27
down sleeping bags, 63, 64–65, 73, 84
draft tubes, 70
dry cleaning, 27, 73
duffel bags, 46
duPont fibers, 64, 65, 66

Eagles Nest Wilderness, 162
El Capitan, 39
Eldorado Mountain, 180–81
elevation gain/loss, 96–97, 100–101
emergencies, 159–61
Emerson, Ralph Waldo, 120
E.M.S., 15
excess baggage charges, 46
extension straps, 39
external-frame packs, 43–44, 45, 47, 48, 49,
    50, 102
eyeglasses, 85

fire, see Campfires
fire hazards, 46, 58, 132–33
fire rings, 122, 128, 129
first-aid, 95, 148–61
fishing, 21
fitness, 101, 116–17, 171
flash floods, 125
fleece garments, 20, 27
floating lids, 50
fly rods, 42
food, 13, 46, 50, 88–95, 101, 139, 140–45,
    159, 168
foot care, 30–32, 34, 70
forest fires, 132–33
Franklin, Benjamin, 171
frostbite, frost nip, 28, 35
fuel, 46, 101, 145–47, 169
fungal infections, 34

gaiters, 25–26, 114, 163; neck, 20
Gatewood, "Grandma," 30
gear, 13–15; see also indiv. items
Gelman, Janet, 47, 48
Giardia lamblia, 151, 152
giardiasis, 151–52
Glacier N.P., 142
Glenn, Steve, 140
gloves, 17, 26, 61, 149, 169
Gore, W. L., 21–22, 23, 27, 59–60
Gore Range, 162–63
Gore-Tex, 21–24, 25, 27, 31, 34, 54,
    59–60, 71
Grand Canyon N.P., 40, 123, 129, 130–31,
    132, 133
Grand Teton N.P., 44
Great Gulf Wilderness, 127
Great Smoky Mountains N.P., 122, 134
gullies, 126

Hackett, Peter, Acute Mountain Sickness . . . ,
    156
hail, 16
Half Dome, 140, 141
hammocks, 128
hand lotion, 102
hats, 17, 20, 149, 155
headlamps, 81–83, 95
heat exhaustion/heatstroke, 154–55
heel lift, 37
High Country News, 182
hiking, 10, 21, 23, 24, 30; long-distance, 50,
    94–95; low-impact, 11, 121–39, 179, 182;
    off–trail, 101, 112, 122
hiking errors, 108, 109–10
hiking tips, 110–13
Himalayas, 37, 51
hip belts, 44, 47–48, 49, 104, 111
hip stabilization straps, 49
Hoechst-Celanese, 65
hold-open bars, 50
Hollofil fibers, 66
hoods, 24
horses, 114
hunters, 33
huts, 168
hypothermia, 153–54

ice axes, 42–43, 86–87, 112
Indian Peaks Wilderness, 16, 113
injection molding, 33–34
insect repellents, 149
insects, see Mosquitoes and biting insects
insulation, 18, 19, 21, 25, 33, 34, 36, 55, 59,
    63–66, 72, 137, 138
internal-frame packs, 43, 44–45, 47, 48–49,
    50, 102
iodine tablets, 152–53

jackets, 17, 19, 21–24, 168
Jensen, Don, 138

Kaelin, Joe, 53, 63–64, 70–71, 88–89
Kansas State University Institute for Envi-
    ronmental Research, 154
Keds sneakers, 30
Kelty packs, 43–44
knives, 17, 84, 151
Komito, Steve, 30, 32

lactic acid buildup, 110
land managers, see Rangers
landmarks, 110
lashing, 86
lashing points, 50
lash patches, 42
leather boots, 29–32, 33–34, 36–37, 38
leather conditioner, 38
lightning storms, 124, 156, 157–58
lip balm, 17, 95
liquid sealants, 30

Lite Loft, 25, 66
litter, see Waste disposal
Little Yosemite Valley, 140–41, 142
L. L. Bean, 15
Logan bread, 94
long-distance trekking, 50, 94–95
long johns, 17, 18, 20
Longs Peak, 24, 81–82
Lost Creek Wilderness, 109
Lowe, Greg, 44
Lowe, Jeff, 24
LTD construction, 24
lumbar packs, pads, 40, 49

maps, 13, 41, 95, 96–100, 104–8, 109, 116, 120,
    159; folding, 118–19; topographical,
    97–100, 106
Maze (Utah), 110
Metcalf, Peter, 68
Micro Loft, 66
Moisture Vapor Transport Rate (MVTR), 22
moleskin, 151
mosquitoes and biting insects, 17, 18, 20, 54,
    128, 148–50
Mount Agassiz, 44
mountaineering, 14, 36–37, 42–43, 44, 161
mountain hiking, 20, 24, 26, 32
Mountain House dinners, 92
mountain sickness, 155–56
Mount Baldy, 100
Mount Deborah, 138
Mount Fay, 53
Mount Hunter, 68
Mount Huntington, 63, 64
Mount McKinley, 29, 47, 48, 58–59, 62, 67, 68,
    79, 84, 92, 131, 145
Mount Rainier N.P., 127, 129
Mount Sanford, 39
MSR stoves, 78
Muir, John, 52, 53
multi-day packs, 43–51
mummy sleeping bags, 69–70

national parks, 104, 117, 120, 121–23
Nike footwear, 34
noise pollution, 133
Northeast, 25
North Pole, 68
Northwest, 25
Nutrasweet Kool–Aid, 152, 153

off-trail hiking, 101, 112, 122
Outward Bound Map and Compass Handbook
    The, 105

pac boots, 32, 33–34, 38, 164
Pacific Crest Trail, 94
Pacific Northwest, 17, 25
Pacific Palisades, 44
pack bags, 50–51
packing errors, 45

packs, 13, 39–51, 64, 85–86, 110, 111, 134, 145, 164; day, 40–43; fanny, 40; multi–day, 43–51; overloading of, 14, 39–40, packing of, 101–4
pack straps, 41
panel-loading packs, 50, 51
pants, 17, 18, 20, 21, 26, 149, 168
parkas, 19, 20, 25, 27, 85
peak-baggers, 42–43
personal hygiene kits, 85
petroglyphs, 110, 120
pets, 117
photography, 17, 26, 40, 50, 69, 80, 83, 95, 113, 117, 120, 132, 133
pile garments, 20–21
pillows, 72
plastic trash, 130
pockets, 21, 24–25, 51, 103
poison ivy, 34
Polarguard fabrics, 25, 65–66
polyester, 18, 19–20, 25, 26, 27, 34
polyolefin, 25
polypropylene, 19, 26, 34
ponchos, 21
postholing, 163
Potable Aqua, 152, 153
pots and pans, 80, 147
Prima Loft, 66

Quallofil, 25, 64, 66

radiant barrier liners, 68–69
rain, 18, 30, 54, 59, 63, 64, 70, 85, 102, 154
rain gear, 13, 16, 19, 20, 21–24, 85, 134
Randall, Cora, 16, 17, 25, 26–27, 28, 35, 47, 67, 71, 72, 80, 90, 91, 94, 109, 113, 145, 147, 151, 152, 176
Randall, Glenn, Cold Comfort, 169
rangers, 101, 114, 115, 123, 132, 140, 141, 143, 144, 152
rapids, 34
ravens, 145
R E.I., 15
repair kits, 84, 85–87, 146
rest, 110
rest step, 110
ripstop repair tape, 62

river-runners, 34, 130–31, 132
Roberts, David, 138
rockfalls, 112
Rocky Mountains, 16–17, 25, 91, 110, 155, 164
Rocky Mountains N.P., 46, 70–71, 81, 88, 115, 122, 123, 129, 131, 132, 139, 142, 163, 173–74
Rosenthal, Sol Roy, 10
running shoes, 29, 30, 35
Ruth Glacier, 63

sandals, 30, 34
sanitation, see Waste disposal
Scotchgard, 23, 38
scrambling, 14, 45, 101
scree, 115
search-and-rescue groups, 101
Second Skin, 151
Seneca, Lucius Annaeus, 95
Sharkey, Brian J., Physiology of Fitness, The, 117
Shenandoah N.P., 122, 123, 129, 134, 142
Shipton, Eric, 61
shirts, 17, 18, 149
shorts, 16, 17–18
shoulder straps, 24, 48–49, 104, 111
shoulder yokes, 48–49
Sierra Mountains, 17, 52, 110, 123
silicone conditioners, 34, 38
silk liner socks, 35, 151
skis, skiing, 10, 14, 21, 39, 42, 44, 45, 84, 85, 101, 110, 164–66, 168–69, 171; cross–country, 163–64, 166
sleeping bags, 51, 53, 63–73, 101, 102, 137–38, 154, 168; care, 72–73, 85; design/fit, 69–71; doublers, 71; down vs. synthetic, 63–66, 178; liners, 68–69; temperature ratings, 66–67
sleeping pads, 71–72, 134, 137
smoking, 101
snakebite, 156–57
sneakers, 13, 30
Sno-Seal, 38
snow, 26, 50, 60, 61, 63, 70, 84, 104, 110, 126, 131, 154, 161, 163–68, 170, 171
snowblindness, 85
snow caves, 167–68
snowfields, 36, 43, 85, 86–87, 112, 115

M O D E R N   B A C K P A C K E R ' S   H A N D B O O K

snowpack, 170, 171
snowshoes, snowshoeing, 21, 33, 45, 84, 101, 110, 163—64, 169
soap, 147
socks, 26, 31, 34, 35, 37, 84, 112, 151
solo wilderness travel, climbing, 101
specialty shops, 14–15, 62, 64
Speedy Stitchers, 47, 86
spindrift, 71
spindrift collars, 50
spring hiking, 171
spur trails, 109
Steger, Will, 68
Stephenson, Jack, 18, 69
Stephenson Warmlite Equipment, 59, 169
sternum straps, 111
stoves, 46, 51, 101, 129, 145–47, 168, 169, 178
Strawberry Peak, 10
stream crossings, 111–12
streamwalking, 34
stuff sacks, 72–73, 84, 102, 134
summer hiking, 13, 16–18, 20, 26, 30, 34, 37, 45, 60, 68, 73, 82, 85, 91, 104, 114, 154
sunburn, 150
sunglasses and goggles, 85
sunscreen, 95, 102–3, 142, 150
sweaters, 13, 19, 101
sweatshirts, 17, 20, 21
Swiss Army knives, 84
synthetic fabrics, 17, 18, 19–20, 25, 27, 35, 63–66, 68; see also indiv.

talus, 44, 115
tarps, 54, 128
technical day packs, 42
Tenth Mountain Division Trail Association, 168
tent poles, 54, 55, 56, 57–58, 59, 61, 62, 95, 136, 138, 166–67, 169
tents, 51, 52–62, 64, 82, 101, 102, 138, 166–68, 169, 178; A-frame, 54–55, 56; care, 61–62, 85; condensation in, 58–60; dome, 56–57; four-season, 60–61; hub, 57–58, 60; hybrid, 60; pitching, 134–37; Praying Mantis, 58; pup, 54–55; pyramid, 55, 56; three-season, 60, 61; tube, 53–54; tunnel, 57, 60; ventilation systems in, 59

Texolite, 68–69
Thayer family, 173–74, 177
theft, 46, 139
Therm-A-Rest mattresses, 72
Thinsulate, 34
Thompson, Benjamin, 20
Thoreau, Henry David, 9, 27, 148
3M fibers, 65, 66
Thuermer, Angus, 63
thunderstorms, 16–17, 21, 22, 24, 125, 134, 157–58
timberline, 21, 50, 85, 115, 122, 134, 154
Todd-Tex, 59
toilet paper, 85, 95, 122
top-loading packs, 50–51
Trails Illustrated, 100
trails: condition, 14, 16, 29, 30, 44, 45, 101, 104–5, 110, 112; distances, 100–101; erosion, 30, 113–14, 115, 122; etiquette, 110, 112, 113–17, 120; multiple, 114
travel packs, 46
Trekking Chef, The, 90
tripods, 42, 45, 50, 102
trowels, 85, 131, 161
T-shirts, 16, 18, 149
Tuoloumne Meadows, 114
turtlenecks, 17, 18, 20

underwear, 26–27; see also Long johns
U.S. Bureau of Land Management, 181
U.S. Forest Service, 181
U.S. Geological Survey, 99–100
urethane-coated fabrics, 21

vapor barrier liners, 68–69
Velcro, 25, 169
"Visqueen burritos," 54
viruses, 153
visual pollution, 133–34
volunteering, 114

walking sticks, 110–11, 163
waste disposal, 85, 122, 130–33, 138–39, 142, 144, 179, 182
watches, 85, 100
water, 124, 126, 133, 147, 151–53, 160–61
water bars, 114

water bottles, 13, 69, 101, 133, 169
water filters, 153
waterproof fabrics, 21–24
waterproofing compounds, 23, 30, 31,
   38
weapons, 117
weather, 17, 18, 22, 25, 34, 37, 40, 50, 58–59,
   68, 79, 153–54
Whillans Box, 61
White Mountains, 115, 127
whiteouts, 116
wicking, 19–20
wilderness: future of, 180–82
Wilderness Act, 181
Wilderness Society, 182

wildlife, 117, 120, 123, 130, 133, 139, 140–4
   181–82
wind, 57, 60, 61, 81, 82, 88, 124, 150, 154, 17
winter camping, 25, 33, 50, 60, 69–70, 85,
   104, 126, 131–32, 137, 153, 162–72
women hikers, 47
wool, 19, 35

Yellowstone N.P., 142, 166
Yosemite N.P., 39, 46, 115, 122–23, 127, 129, 139,
   140–41, 142, 152
yurts, 168

zippers, 62, 70, 71, 168–69
Z-liner construction, 24